Mustafa.

بسم الله الرحمن الرحيم

Abdul Raheem

The Messenger of Virtue ﷺ

FORTY REASONS WHY THE MESSENGER OF ALLĀH ﷺ WAS FAVOURED OVER THE OTHER PROPHETS عليهم السلام

The Messenger of Virtue ﷺ

FORTY REASONS WHY THE MESSENGER OF ALLĀH ﷺ WAS FAVOURED OVER THE OTHER PROPHETS عليهم السلام

A Commentary on The Beginning of the Quest for the High Esteem of the Messenger ﷺ

SHAYKH ABDUL RAHEEM LIMBADA

ḥafiẓahullāh

Tafseer Raheemi Publications

تفسير رحيمي

First Edition: November 2017

ISBN: 978-1-912301-06-5

Published by:

Tafseer Raheemi Publications www.tafseer-raheemi.com

Author	Shaykh Abdul Raheem Limbada
Editing & Typesetting	Mufti Abdus Subhan Dalvi
Cover Design	Shaykh Ahmed *ibn* Shaykh Mohammed Patel
Printed by	Imak Ofset, Istanbul (imakofset.com.tr)

Available to purchase from www.tafseer-raheemi.com/shop

Correspondence to the author or publishers may be sent to: info@tafseer-raheemi.com

وأحسن منك لم تر قط عيني

وأجمل منك لم تلد النساء

خلقت مبرأ من كل عيب

كأنك قد خلقت كما تشاء

My eyes have not seen anything more beautiful than him
No women has borne such perfection
You were created free from all deficiencies
It is as though you were created as you wished

Ḥassān ibn Thābit رضي الله عنه

Contents

Foreword

بِسْمِ اللَّهِ الرَّحْمَٰنِ الرَّحِيمِ

IN THE NAME OF ALLĀH, the Most Merciful and compassionate. I bear witness that there is no god but Allāh alone, without partners and that Muḥammad is His servant and messenger. Thereafter, I invoke the blessings of Allāh and peace upon His final Messenger, Muḥammad, his Family and companions, along with all those who follow them in goodness till the Day of Rising.

The book in your possession is a culmination of two courses delivered by our respected teacher on *Bidāyah as-Sūl fī Tafḍīl ar-Rasūl* at our request. One session was delivered at Imperial University and the other was University of Lancashire. When we requested our respected teacher to take some time out of his busy schedule to deliver the course, he instantly obliged. When he found out the course revolved around the *sīrah*, he uttered, "when and where?" without any hesitation. This was only because of his love for the Prophet ﷺ that he never misses an opportunity to speak about him - the Beloved of Allāh; the Interceder on the Day where no intercession will be accepted; The Final Prophet ﷺ.

I am not a scholar by whose recommendation a publication is taken into consideration but having sat at these two courses and witnessed our respected teacher teach the course, I can say that the same passion has become imbued with the book. Thus, if you were unable to attend the lectures, the knowledge contained herein will benefit you immensely in this world and the next.

After thanking Allāh ﷻ and our respected teacher, I would like to thank Muftī Abdus Subhan who meticulously transcribed the course notes and then edited them thereafter. May Allāh ﷻ reward them both in this world and the next. May He also make this publication a means of our salvation and intercession for us on the Day of Rising. *Āmīn.*

YAHYA BATHA
Turath Publishing
13th Muḥarram 1439 | 4th October 2017

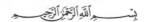

Editor's Preface

بِسْمِ اللهِ الرَّحْمٰنِ الرَّحِيْمِ

IN THE NAME OF ALLĀH, the All Merciful, the Most Merciful. We praise Him and we invoke blessings upon His Noble Messenger, Muḥammad ﷺ, the Seal of the Prophets.

The Messenger of Allāh ﷺ has almost become like a stranger to us. At worst, many from within our community view him with negativity due to various portrayals presented by his critics. As a result, they close their minds towards him without distinguishing spurious narratives and subsequently go on to live lives bereft of perfect guidance.

In contrast, there are others within the community who have studied the biography of the Noble Prophet ﷺ and endeavour to follow his blessed Sunnah. Many books have been authored wherein his blessed characteristics have been deliberated upon, thus providing a framework for those who are ardent to follow. Such fervour in emulating him is commendable and not without its benefit or due reward.

However, if one truly wishes to develop their recognition of the Messenger of Allāh ﷺ, it is necessary for them to study him in the context of his closest comparisons – the prophets of Allāh عليهم السلام. It becomes apparent quite imminently that the Messenger of Allāh ﷺ was granted great superiority and virtue by Allāh ﷻ over the rest of creation.

The publication in your possession attempts to shed light on this particular point and by studying it, you will be able to recognise the magnificent status of the Messenger of Allāh ﷺ.

The book in itself is a commentary to the famous '*Bidāyah as-Sūl fī Tafḍīl ar-Rasūl – The Beginning of the Quest for the High Esteem of the Messenger* ﷺ'. A son who was desirous to know more about the Messenger of Allāh ﷺ sought information from his father, Shaykh ʿIzz ad-Dīn ibn ʿAbd as-Salām رحمه الله, and as a result, the latter dictated approximately forty points as to why the Noble Prophet ﷺ was favoured over the rest of humanity. Similarly, presented before you in this publication is a commentary of the aforementioned points which was dictated to me by my spiritual father and revered teacher, Shaykh al-Ḥadīth Abdul Raheem ibn Shaykh Dāwūd (may Allāh ﷻ protect him).

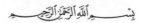

My beloved friend, Yahya Batha, had organised a course at a London university wherein Shaykh Abdul Raheem was invited to deliver a seminar on the aforementioned book which had, at that time, just been published by Turath Publishing. This happened approximately seven to eight years ago and was the subject of much interest. Many are aware that Shaykh travels the world regularly and is often invited to give sermons in various countries; however, this was not the case several years ago. Shaykh Abdul Raheem would seldom visit London and so when Turath Publishing had advertised the course, there was a plethora of interest – for Londoners, it is not everyday that they get to study with a scholar of ḥadīth. The course was highly successful and well received by those who attended.

Now, it is mysterious how Allāh ﷻ works and how He places ideas and determination within the breasts of men. Likewise, it is bewildering how one can be lazy towards such impulses and fail to recognise and discern Divine guidance when it grips them. To this date, I cannot recall what gave me the impetus to jot down Shaykh's words; I remember myself lost in thought one day only to find a growing inner determination to put pen to paper. At this point, I was a student of the ʿAlimiyyah programme where my teacher, Maulānā Usman Ali (may Allāh ﷻ protect him), would say, "A good idea is from Allāh ﷻ, if you honour and implement it, Allāh ﷻ will place more ideas within your heart. If you ignore and belittle it, such ideas will cease." Thus I opened up my original notes, recordings of Shaykh's sessions, and locked myself in a room with a new notepad. Alḥamdulillāh, the notes were completed within a few months and the printed document was a verbatim copy of Shaykh Abdul Raheem's lesson. I was in regular contact with Shaykh Abdul Raheem, who had taken a strong liking to me, and so I sent him the document.

He was extremely pleased with the work and highlighted that he had never imagined that such a thing would be done. I was given much affection and a bottle of ʿitr for my efforts as Shaykh told me he would review the notes. After sometime, Shaykh had sent me his edited version of the notes which he had revised and added to. He instructed me to edit the work as the transcript contained repetitive speech, symptomatic of spoken language. At times during his lesson, Shaykh would make a point but repeat it in several ways with various examples in order to allow even the less knowledgeable to understand. Likewise, he also asked me to rephrase various passages to maintain literary fluidity and bear clear meaning. However, I became lazy.

As days passed by, day to day businesses increased and the responsibility of editing the book changed hands rapidly. However, nothing categorical was being done – a point which Shaykh would raise with myself and Yahya Batha from time to time. At this point, I should highlight (and I am sure that others will agree) that Shaykh Abdul Raheem's character and mannerisms are phenomenal. He would never scold us for our failure to complete the work but rather, he would playfully tease us. I remember whilst being a student in Dār al-Iftā, I left the premises to return home without permission due to some emergency. I did message Shaykh Abdul Raheem but was incredibly worried about being scolded. I returned a day later and was collected from the train station by my beloved classmate, Muftī Ibrahim Saeed al-Makkī and I highlighted my qualms to him. He said something profound: "Why are you so worried? There is not a softer person in Darul Uloom than him! He will never embarrass any student." Upon my return, Shaykh did not reprimand me but reminded me of following protocol and then resumed his regular display of affection.

Thus, the document was left unedited for several years until a couple of months ago when I visited Shaykh at his residence in Bolton. I was in attendance at a wedding which was only a mile away and so I decided to visit Shaykh. We spoke for some time about a variety of matters when he took out a folder with the papers that I instantly recognised as the transcript of his course. Shaykh advised me to finish editing it and so I returned to London, eager to fulfil his wish.

How strange is it that many years later I have edited Shaykh's words sitting in the very room that I had initially jotted everything down in? It started as a good idea which I became lazy with, but when Allāh ﷻ wills for something to happen, there is not a power strong enough to deter it. This is why I say that it is mysterious how Allāh ﷻ works and how He places ideas and determination within the breasts of men. Likewise, it is bewildering how one can be lazy towards such impulses and fail to recognise and discern Divine guidance when it grips them.

By the grace of Allāh ﷻ, the work was completed within a month. To highlight Shaykh ʿIzz ad-Dīn's ؒ points, his speech has been printed in bold in order to distinguish the *matn* (core text) from Shaykh Abdul Raheem's commentary. Likewise, the Arabic text of the *matn* can be found towards the end of the book. It should also be recognised that the English translation of Shaykh ʿIzz ad-Dīn's ؒ words have been taken directly from the book, *'The Beginning of the Quest for the High Esteem of the*

Messenger ﷺ' which was published by Ustādha Aisha Bewley through Turath Publishing.

I would like to thank my dear friends, Maulana Abdullah Patel and Maulana Ahmed Patel for their valuable help and input. They made themselves available whenever I called upon them and responded with great suggestions.

I pray to Allāh ﷻ that He accepts this work from Shaykh Abdul Raheem and all those who have given time to it. May He grant us sincerity, faith and the strength to help us commit ourselves to good works and noble causes. *Āmīn.*

ABDUS SUBHAN DALVI
Lecturer of Ḥadīth
Azhar Academy, London
23rd Shaʿbān 1438 | 30th May 2016

Introduction

بِسْمِ ٱللَّهِ ٱلرَّحْمَٰنِ ٱلرَّحِيمِ

ALL PRAISE IS FOR ALLĀH ﷻ ALONE, Lord of the universe and may the choicest of blessings be upon our Master, our Beloved, Muḥammad al-Muṣṭafā, as well as his family, his companions and all those who have followed in their footsteps.

Without any doubt, the Messenger of Allāh ﷺ is the best among the creation of Allāh ﷻ. He was the one who was the most acquainted with those matters that please Allāh ﷻ and as to those things that anger Him. He was the most cautious in observing his duties to Allāh ﷻ and fulfilling His rights. He was the most obedient to Allāh ﷻ, the most in showing his reliance upon Allāh ﷻ, the most in worship to Allāh ﷻ and he was the most fearful of Him. Indeed, he had the most love for his Creator.

With regards to his need for Allāh ﷻ, he would supplicate, "O Allāh! It is Your mercy that I hope for, do not put me in charge of my *nafs* for a blink of an eye, otherwise I would be drawn closer towards evil and I would be distanced from virtue." He would supplicate, "O Turner of the hearts, set my heart upon Your Dīn and O Manager of the hearts, turn my heart towards Your obedience."

When expressing his love for Allāh ﷻ, he would say, "O Allāh! Make your love dearer to me than myself, my family and dearer [to me] than a chilled drink on a hot day."

He would stand worshipping Allāh ﷻ for hours during the nightly prayers until his feet would swell. When he was asked as to why he exerts himself so much despite being pardoned for his past and future mistakes, he responded, "Should I not then be a grateful servant?"

He would fast every Monday and Thursday, most of the month of *Shaʿbān*, along with the entirety of *Ramaḍān*. He would never hesitate to spend upon the poor. In truth, he was the most generous person to have set foot on the face of the Earth.

As for his fear of Allāh ﷻ, he would implore, "O Allāh! Make Your love the most beloved of all things to me, and make Your fear [and reverence] the most fearful thing in my mind." Sometimes during his night prayers, he would weep excessively to the extent that his chest would sound like a boiling kettle.

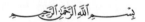

He would seek forgiveness for any misgivings one hundred times in a single day, sometimes in one sitting, all in order to show his appreciation and respect to Allāh ﷻ. He himself would say, "My Lord educated me and He educated me very well. My Lord taught me manners and He refined me very well."

Throughout his blessed life, we are able to observe how he would interact with his Lord ﷻ. After the incident of *Ṭā'if*, where he was beaten to the extent that his bleeding caused his blessed feet to stick to his slippers. He had somehow retreated to a secure place where he fainted. When he came to his senses he supplicated with words that brought the mercy of Allāh ﷻ into motion. He exclaimed,

> *"O Allāh! To You do I relate the weakness of my strength, the lack of my planning and my fallen status in the eyes of people. O the Most Merciful from amongst those who show mercy! You are the Lord of the weak and You are my Lord - to whom do You hand me over? To someone distant? One who will attack me? Or to some enemy in whose hands You have placed my affairs? If You are not angry with me then I need not worry, however, Your [given] security is more encompassing for me. I seek refuge in the Light of Your countenance by which all darkness lightens up, and upon which depends the matters of the world and the Hereafter, from Your wrath befalling me or that You become displeased with me. It is Your right that forgiveness be sought from You until You are pleased. There is neither power to turn away from evil nor any strength to do good except with Your [given] guidance."*

Let us ponder; had we been vilified and attacked in such a savage manner, we would have complained about Allāh ﷻ within our circles. Our state has become such that we criticise Him upon the smallest of problems and refuse to acknowledge the plethora of virtues He has bestowed upon us.

Once a desert dweller came to the Messenger of Allāh ﷺ and said, "We supplicate to Allāh ﷻ through you, and to you through Allāh ﷻ." The Messenger of Allāh ﷺ started quivering and thereafter remarked, "May Allāh ﷻ have mercy on you. Surely Allāh cannot be asked to request someone for something. Do you know who Allāh is? His Throne is in the skies like this." He then gestured by making a circle with his hand reminiscent of a dome.

He taught us that the best form of seeking forgiveness is by supplicating, "O Allāh! You are my Lord, there is no deity besides You, You created me, I am Your slave, and

I remain upon Your covenant as to the best of my ability. I seek Your refuge from the evils that I have committed. I acknowledge Your favours upon me and I admit to my mistakes, so forgive me because none can forgive sins besides You."

A person cannot be respectful towards the Creator unless he is respectful to the creation. When we study the conduct of the Messenger of Allāh ﷺ within his community, we recognise his noble mannerisms. He would never bellow, nor would he rebuke people and he would object to being rude or vulgar. He would exude great levels of modesty and would refrain from stretching his legs towards someone in a gathering. When he would arrive in a gathering, he would sit wherever there was an empty space. He would not look for the best seat and nor would he make someone stand up from their place in order to make it his own.

He would always lower his gaze and would never stare at the skies. He would remain cheerful, even though he might be hiding many agonies. He would always be smiling and maintained a great sense of humour.

Allāh, the Almighty, has full knowledge of everything; He knew the nature of His beloved ﷺ and due to his sublime characteristics, Allāh ﷻ bestowed upon him the loftiest position among the creation. Allāh ﷻ has proclaimed whilst undertaking an oath, "You [O Muḥammad] are of a sublime character." If we were to adapt to his lifestyle, and inculcate the same qualities within us, we would also become beloved to Allāh ﷻ.

The brief treatise in front of you discusses some of the special attributes of the Messenger of Allāh. It was dictated by Shaykh ʿIzz ad-Dīn ibn ʿAbd al-Salām رحمه الله upon the request of his son.

The commentary of the book is also a dictation; my dearest and respected friend, Yaḥya Batha, who is the founder and chairman of Turāth publications, had organised two seminars for the study of the aforementioned treatise. The first seminar was held in London and the other in Preston. Both events were recorded and uploaded on to YouTube with the title *'In Search of the Prophet'* and *'In Praise of the Chosen Prophet'* respectively.

Thereafter, Muftī Abdus Subḥān Dalvi, who is the most dearest to me, put pen to paper and noted down the commentary from the recordings. I had never thought that this would materialise. However, he did the work at an amazing speed. In fact, I feel ashamed that I was bit lax in proof reading. However, when Allāh ﷻ intends to do something, nothing can stop Him. All praise is for Allāh, it is now in front of you in the form of a book.

My sincere prayers are with those who offered their help in any way in publishing this humble work. May Allāh ﷻ reward them all in full, fulfil their needs of this world as well as the Hereafter. *Āmīn*.

ABDUL RAHEEM
A Servant of Dar al-ʿUlūm al-ʿArabiyyah al-Islamiyyah
Bury, UK

الحمد لله نحمده و نستعيينه و نستغفره و نؤمن به و نتوكّل عليه و نعوذ بالله من شرور انفسنا و من سيّئات اعمالنا من يّهده الله فلا مضلّ له و من يّضلله فلا هادى له ، و نشهد ان لّا اله الا الله وحده لا شريك له و نشهد انّ سيّدناو نبيّنا و شفيعنا و حبيبنا و سندنا و مولانا محمّدا عبده و رسوله ، صلى الله تبارك وتعالى عليه و على اله و صحبه و بارك و سلّم تسليما كثيرا،

امّا بعد: فَاَعُوْذُ بِاللهِ مِنَ الْشَّيْطَانِ الرَّجِيْمِ ، بِسْمِ اللَّهِ الرَّحْمَٰنِ الرَّحِيمِ

تِلْكَ الرُّسُلُ فَضَّلْنَا بَعْضَهُمْ عَلَىٰ بَعْضٍ ۘ مِّنْهُم مَّن كَلَّمَ اللَّهُ ۖ وَرَفَعَ بَعْضَهُمْ دَرَجَاتٍ ۚ وَآتَيْنَا عِيسَى ابْنَ مَرْيَمَ الْبَيِّنَاتِ وَأَيَّدْنَاهُ بِرُوحِ الْقُدُسِ

و قال تعالى: آمَنَ الرَّسُولُ بِمَا أُنزِلَ إِلَيْهِ مِن رَّبِّهِ وَالْمُؤْمِنُونَ ۚ كُلٌّ آمَنَ بِاللَّهِ وَمَلَائِكَتِهِ وَكُتُبِهِ وَرُسُلِهِ لَا نُفَرِّقُ بَيْنَ أَحَدٍ مِّن رُّسُلِهِ ۚ وَقَالُوا سَمِعْنَا وَأَطَعْنَا ۖ غُفْرَانَكَ رَبَّنَا وَإِلَيْكَ الْمَصِيرُ لَا يُكَلِّفُ اللَّهُ نَفْسًا إِلَّا وُسْعَهَا ۚ لَهَا مَا كَسَبَتْ وَعَلَيْهَا مَا اكْتَسَبَتْ ۗ رَبَّنَا لَا تُؤَاخِذْنَا إِن نَّسِينَا أَوْ أَخْطَأْنَا ۚ رَبَّنَا وَلَا تَحْمِلْ عَلَيْنَا إِصْرًا كَمَا حَمَلْتَهُ عَلَى الَّذِينَ مِن قَبْلِنَا ۚ رَبَّنَا وَلَا تُحَمِّلْنَا مَا لَا طَاقَةَ لَنَا بِهِ ۖ وَاعْفُ عَنَّا وَاغْفِرْ لَنَا وَارْحَمْنَا ۚ أَنتَ مَوْلَانَا فَانصُرْنَا عَلَى الْقَوْمِ الْكَافِرِينَ

و قال تعالى: وَلَوْلَا فَضْلُ اللَّهِ عَلَيْكَ وَرَحْمَتُهُ لَهَمَّت طَّائِفَةٌ مِّنْهُمْ أَن يُضِلُّوكَ وَمَا يُضِلُّونَ إِلَّا أَنفُسَهُمْ ۖ وَمَا يَضُرُّونَكَ مِن شَيْءٍ ۚ وَأَنزَلَ اللَّهُ عَلَيْكَ الْكِتَابَ وَالْحِكْمَةَ وَعَلَّمَكَ مَا لَمْ تَكُن تَعْلَمُ ۚ وَكَانَ فَضْلُ اللَّهِ عَلَيْكَ عَظِيمًا

و قال النّبي صلى الله عليه و سلّم: انّما انا رحمة مهداة

و قال النّبي صلى الله عليه و سلّم: فضلت على الانبياء بست: اوتيت جوامع الكلم و نصرت بالرعب وأحلت لي الغنائم وجعلت لي الأرض مسجدا وطهورا و كان النّبى يبعث الى قومه خاصة و ارسلت الى

الخلق كافة و ختم بى النبيون، صدق الله مولانا العظيم ، و صدق رسوله النّبى الكريم ، و نحن على ما قال رّبنا و خالقنا و رازقنا من الْشّاهدين و الْشَاكرين و الحمد لله ربّ العالمين ،

إِنَّ اللَّهَ وَمَلَائِكَتَهُ يُصَلُّونَ عَلَى النَّبِيِّ ۚ يَا أَيُّهَا الَّذِينَ آمَنُوا صَلُّوا عَلَيْهِ وَسَلِّمُوا تَسْلِيمًا

اللّٰهمّ صلِّ على محمّد و على ال محمّد كما صلّيت على ابراهيم انّك حميد مجيد ، اللّٰهمّ بارك على محمّد و على ال محمّد كما باركت على ابراهيم انّك حميد مجيد ،محمّد سيّد الكونين و الثّقلين و الفريقين من عرب و من عجم ، نبيّنا الآمر النّاهى فلا احد ابرّ فى قول لا منه و لا نعم

فاق النّبيّينا فى خلق و فى خلق و لم يدانوه فى علم وّ لا كرم

دع ما ادّعته النصارى فى نبيّهم و احكم بما شئت مدحا فيه و احتكم

فانّ فضل رسول الله ليس له حدّ فيعرب عنه ناطق بفم

Session One

Introduction to Bidāyah as-Sūl fī Tafḍīl ar-Rasūl

MY RESPECTED ELDERS, dearest friends, brothers and sisters; first of all, most of us who are sitting here are Muslims and we believe in the Messenger of Allāh ﷺ as our prophet. Therefore, whenever the following verse is recited in front of you, your lips should immediately move in invoking salutations upon the Messenger of Allāh ﷺ:

> *"Surely, Allāh and His angels send blessings to the Prophet. O you who believe, do pray Allāh to bless him, and send your ṣalām (prayer for his being in peace) to him in Abūndance."*[1]

The Messenger of Allāh ﷺ has said, "Whosoever sends one salutation upon me, Allāh showers ten blessings upon him."[2]

Thus, it is for one's own benefit that when the Messenger of Allāh's ﷺ name is mentioned in their presence, they at least recite, '*salallāhu ʿalayhi wa sallam*' or the invocation which we recite in prayer. May Allāh ﷻ give us the ability to do so (*Amīn*).

Like Dr. ʿImrān before me, I would also like to thank you for your attendance today. The more we learn about the Noble Messenger ﷺ, the more we develop and increase in love and affection for him. We understand what a magnificent person he was. He was not merely an ordinary person, but rather, he was a special, unique person. He was the Messenger of Allāh ﷻ and a prophet! Hence, when we acknowledge this, we are able to ascertain that whatever he does or articulates is not on his own accord - it is from Allāh ﷻ. Each moment of his noble life was guided by Allāh ﷻ. Even after his demise, Allāh ﷻ protected his honour, and the religion he bought.

Accordingly, when we understand the value of the Messenger of Allāh ﷺ, we are able to develop love for him. Once again, it is only for our own benefit and it is for this reason that I thank you for your attendance.

Throughout the day, I will navigate our discussion through various topics *in-shā-Allāh*. In the first session, we will attempt to discuss the name of the book which is to

---

[1] Al-Qur'ān 33:56

[2] Ṣaḥīḥ Muslim

be studied. Thereafter, we will also deliberate upon the topic of giving preference to some prophets over others and as to whether it is permissible to do so. We will analyse the Sharia ruling pertaining to the statement, 'so-and-so prophet is better than so-and-so prophet' and its like. Finally, we will describe the Messenger of Allāh ﷺ through his attributes and qualities.

The book we are studying is a brief treatise which was dictated by the author to his son. It is for this reason that it has been documented in such an informal way. The son had asked his father, "Inform me of the special attributes of the Messenger of Allāh ﷺ. In what ways did Allāh ﷻ give superiority to the Messenger of Allāh ﷺ over the other prophets?" Consequently, the father began his discourse and within a short period of time, he had dictated forty different reasons as to why the Messenger of Allāh ﷺ was given preference over the other prophets. This was done from his memory and this is what has been documented in this book.

The name of the book which we have in front of us is '*Bidāyah as-Sūl fī Tafḍīl ar-Rasūl* – The Beginning of the Quest for the High Esteem of the Messenger ﷺ'. The word '*Bidāyah*' is a variation taken from the word '*ibtidā*'' which means 'a beginning'. It is possible that the author may have intended to use the lexis, '*Bidāyat*' from '*bidā*'' which means 'to appear'. Thus, the title would then be translated as, 'The Materialisation of Questions Pertaining to the Superiority of the Messenger'. The word '*As-Sūl*' comes from the lexis '*Su'āl*' which means to 'question'. At this juncture, a question may arise as to why this query appeared in the mind of the questioner? There must have been some reason. Perhaps, it appeared to him that he should ask his father about 'the Superiority of the Messenger'. We could extend the motive of this question by highlighting that the intended query may have been, 'why was the Messenger of Allāh ﷺ given virtue and excellence over the other prophets?' At this point, we must underline for our non-Muslim friends who are in attendance the concept of a *rasūl*. The word '*rasūl*' is translated as 'messenger'. The author of *Sharḥ al-ʿAqā'id an-Nasafiah* further elaborates in defining the term 'messenger' by saying, "A messenger is a human being whom Allāh ﷻ has sent to the creation in order to promulgate His Commands."

It is important to analyse this statement in assessing the criteria for a messenger. Firstly, the given defintion highlights that a messenger will only be selected from humankind; therefore, all other creations inclding the *jinn* and angels are excluded from taking on this mantle.

Secondly, Allāh ⬡ sent messengers to the creation as a means of guidance. The messenger would deliver His commands, legislations and the message with which he was entrusted to the people.

The Creation of Ādam ⬡

At this point, it is relevant to mention the number of prophets that were sent by Allāh ⬡. It is important to remember that the first messenger, Ādam ⬡, was the first man to have ever traversed the earth. The Noble Prophet ⬡ was once asked, 'O Messenger of Allāh, was Ādam a prophet?" He replied, "Most certainly! He was not just a prophet but he was a prophet with whom Allāh spoke." Ādam ⬡ was created in *Jannah*, in the gardens high above the heavens. Allāh ⬡ took various portions of soil from the earth which were differed in toughness and complexing. From these substances, He formed a mould and thereafter created a human being who was 60 ft tall. The creation was then left in that state for some years. The angels would visit this new creation in order to see what was being created by Allāh ⬡. Likewise, Shayṭān, who at that point, was also in *Jannah* and busy worshipping Allāh ⬡, was also given the freedom to roam and see this new creation.

Infact, in some narrations it is described that he kicked the body of Ādam ⬡ and began to envy him. Thereafter, Allāh ⬡ ordered the soul to enter the mould and this is the very same entity which is extracted from the body of a human being when they meets their end. Thus, the soul was sent down and it entered the body of Ādam ⬡ from his nose, mouth, ears and then proceeded to the rest of his body. When it reached his throat, he opened his eyes and began to observe his surroundings. When it reached his hips, Ādam ⬡ he attempted to stand up. It had not reached his feet before he had sat up and attempted to walk. Allāh ⬡ has indicated to this in the Qur'ān when He said: *"Man is made of haste."*[1]

This verse highlights that man is hasty in his nature and naturally rushes into things. It was only when the soul reached the feet of Ādam ⬡ that he stood up and began to walk.

---

[1] Al-Qur'ān 21:37

Ādam 🌸 was the first person to be created by Allāh 🌸. Further details of the narration mentioned above can be found in biographical and historical books. It has aslo been related by Ibn Kathīr in his book *Qaṣaṣ al-Anbiya*. Thus, Allāh 🌸 kept Ādam 🌸 in Jannah and conversed with him directly, He said: *"O Ādam, dwell you and your wife in Paradise; and eat at pleasure wherever you like, but do not go near this tree, otherwise you will be (counted) among the transgressors."*[1]

Ādam 🌸 acted upon the Command of Allāh 🌸, however, human beings are forgetful. After a period of time, he forgot what he was instructed with and made a mistake; he had eaten from the tree and therefore had to come down to this earth.

As time passed and as humanity progressed, there came a community of people who moved away from the religion that was given to Ādam 🌸 and they invented different things. Shayṭān was known as the infamous enemy of Ādam who had sworn to misguide Ādam's 🌸 progeny till the Day of Standing. Thus, he worked tirelessly in order to mislead people and eventually started getting some success. Consequently, there was a need to guide people and bring them back upon the Straight Path, the teachings that were given to Ādam 🌸. It was at this juncture that Allāh 🌸 sent prophets. Ādam 🌸 had passed away and among his sons was a prophet called Shīsh 🌸. Thus, Allāh taught humanity various lessons through Shīsh 🌸; they were taught how to live and dwell within this world, how to make clothes, how to cover oneself, how to read and write and in this manner, humanity progressed.

Thereafter, Nūḥ 🌸 was sent as a prophet and we are well aware of the story of the Ark. As time progressed, prophets such as Ṣaliḥ, Hūd, Shuʿaib 🌸 emerged until the coming of Ibrāhīm 🌸, the Friend of Allāh 🌸. After Ibrāhīm 🌸, prophets were sent but they all came from his progeny and thus, the prophets that followed were his descendants. He had two sons by the name of Ismaʿīl and Isḥāq 🌸 and from the latter, came many prophets. However, Muḥammad 🌸, the Seal of the Prophets, came from Ismāʿīl 🌸.

We know the names of many from among the prophets, like Ibrāhīm, Mūsā, Sulaimān, Dāwūd and ʿĪsā 🌸 but there are many regarding whom we know nothing about. Allāh 🌸 says in the Qur'an: *"We had sent messengers before you. Among them there*

---

[1] Al-Qur'ān 2:35

are those whose story We have narrated to you, and of them there are those whose story We did not narrate to you."[1]

The Difference Between a Rasūl and a Nabī

There is much discrepancy surrounding the number of prophets that have been sent by Allāh ﷻ. There is some indication as to their number in a ḥadīth narrated on the authority of Abū Dharr al-Ghifārī ؓ in the *Musnad* of Īmām Aḥmad ibn Ḥanbal ؒ. Even though the narration itself is weak in its authenticity, it gives some indication as to the amount of prophets sent by Allāh ﷻ.

Abū Dharr al-Ghifārī ؓ asked, "O Messenger of Allāh, what is the total number of prophets sent by Allāh ﷻ?" He replied, "One hundred and twenty four thousand." Abū Ḍharr ؓ asked, "How many were messengers from among them?" He replied, "Three hundred and thirteen were messengers." This indicates that there is a slight difference between a prophet and a messenger.

A messenger is of a higher rank, whereas a prophet is someone who was not given a book or a new law. It was necessary for the latter to follow the Sharia of another messenger. For example, Mūsā ؑ is a messenger but his diciple Yūshaᶜ ibn Nūn ؑ is a prophet; thus he would have to follow the Sharia of Mūsā ؑ.

Can One Favour a Prophet Over Another?

A topic that can be further elaborated upon is whether it is permissible to grant superiority to one prophet over another. Allāh ﷻ highlights in the Qur'ān: *"We do not differentiate between any of His messengers."*[2]

An incident occurred in Madīnah wherein a complaint was brought to the Messenger of Allāh ﷺ regarding a Jewish man who had set up his stall besides a Muslim man's stall. They engaged in a discussion and for some reason, the Jew remarked, "[I take an oath] by He who favoured Mūsā over the entire universe!" The Muslim who was beside him became infuriated by this statement and as a result, slapped him! He then reprimanded him, "O filth! Do you say he was given preference

[1] Al-Qur'ān 40:78

[2] Al-Qur'ān 2:285

over Muḥammad ﷺ?!" The Jewish man began to weep and came to the Messenger of Allāh ﷺ enquiring as to why he had been hit. The Messenger of Allāh ﷺ then proclaimed, "Do not give me superiority over the prophets [and in another transmission, he said: Do not choose me over Mūsa]." He then went onto say,

> *"People will faint on the Day of Standing and will then regain consciousness. I will be the first to do so and I will see that Mūsā will be holding onto the leg of the Throne of Allāh ﷻ. I do not know if he was among those who fainted and gained consciousness before me or whether he was from those who didn't faint initially. Allāh ﷻ may have saved him because of the unconsciousness that he had suffered upon Mount Ṭūr. [Thus], he would have virtue over me if he came to his senses before me or if he did not lose consciousness. [Therefore] do not give me virtue over Mūsa."*[1]

In this narration, the Messenger of Allāh ﷺ exclaimed, "Do not give me superiority over the prophets [and in another narration, he said, 'Do not choose me over Mūsa']." Hence, it appears that that it is prohibited to favour one prophet over another.

At this juncture, an objection arises as another ḥadīth highlights that the Messenger of Allāh ﷺ said, "I am the leader of the Children of Ādam and this is no boast." This appears to contradict the ḥadiths mentioned above which highlight that the prophets should not be favoured over one another. The scholars have explained the conflicting narrations in the following manner:

The Messenger of Allāh ﷺ had perhaps said, "Do not choose me over Mūsā" before being informed that he is the leader of the Children of Ādam.

i. He had told his community not to favour him over Mūsā ﷺ out of good etiquette and humility.
ii. The Messenger of Allāh ﷺ was simply prohibiting favouring some prophets in such a way that disrespectfully diminishes the status of another.
iii. The Messenger of Allāh ﷺ was simply prohibiting favouring some prophets over others in such a way that causes mischief and violence.
iv. The superiority given to the Messenger of Allāh ﷺ is specific to his prophethood as there can be no comparison. However, things such as virtues and specialisms (i.e. special endowments from Allāh ﷻ) may be compared.

However, on the contrary, there are various verses of the Qur'ān which are

---

[1] Ṣaḥīḥ al-Bukḥārī & Ṣaḥīḥ Muslim

indicative towards the virtue of some prophets and their superiority over others. From among them, some gained closer proximity to their Creator and were more beloved to Allāh 🌼 than others. This is quite simply a fact and there is no question regarding it. This notion is found throughout the Qur'ān as Allāh 🌼 mentions some prophets affectionately and as a result, narrates their stories as often as He can.

Notable Prophets of Allāh 🌼

This point can be examplified by the relationship Mūsā 🌼 enjoys with Allāh 🌼. It is evident that Allāh 🌼 loves Mūsā 🌼 and He regularly mentions him in a variety of chapters. Some commentators of the Qur'ān have articulated that out of the thirty parts, Allāh 🌼 has mentioned Mūsā 🌼 in twenty eight, in some capacity. Consequently, there are only two parts where Mūsā 🌼 is not mentioned.

It is also evident that Allāh 🌼 loves Ibrāhīm 🌼; He mentions Ibrāhīm 🌼 with great affection and mentions his high rank. It is for this reason that the Noble Prophet 🌼 would also narrate stories of Ibrāhīm 🌼 in a beautiful and humble manner. Allāh 🌼 said: *"Indeed, Ibrāhīm was very tender-hearted, very forbearing."*[1]

Allāh 🌼 has also mentioned the attributes of other prophets. About Nūḥ 🌼, Allāh 🌼 said: *"Surely, He was a very grateful servant"*[2]

There is a narration[3] detailing a meeting between Ādam 🌼 and Mūsā 🌼. This incident occurred in the Realm of the Spirits, or perhaps after Mūsā 🌼 had passed away. In the account, Mūsā 🌼 said to Ādam 🌼, "O Ādam! You are of such a high status that Allāh created you with His own Hands, He chose you over the creation and He let you stay in *Jannah*. Despite this, you ate from the tree and brought us all down into this world." Ādam 🌼 replied, "This calamity was in my destiny and so I had no power to avoid it." At this point, I am only trying to highlight the qualities of Ādam 🌼 as thereafter Allāh 🌼 intervened and said, "O Mūsā! Other human beings were created throught cycle of creation but Ādam, *I created him with My own Hands.*"[4]

The angels and *jinns* were created by the command, 'Be, and it comes to be' but as highlighted by the previous verse, Ādam 🌼 was given a special honour. However, it

---

[1] Al-Qur'ān 9:114
[2] Al-Qur'ān 17:3
[3] Ṣaḥīḥ al-Bukhārī
[4] Al-Qur'ān 38:75

should be noted that Allāh 🌸 knows best as to what is intended by the term 'My own Hands'. The ḥadīth continues but it is not relevant from here onwards.

Furthermore, Allāh 🌸 mentions ʿĪsā 🌸 in many places throughout the Qur'ān. He said: *"Surely, the case of ʿĪsā 🌸, in the sight of Allāh, is like the case of Ādam. He created him from soil, then He said to him, 'Be' and he came to be."*[1] Allāh 🌸 has expressed this similitude because ʿĪsā 🌸 was born to only a mother named Maryam 🌸. Allāh 🌸 had sent the Angel Jibrīl 🌸, who stood at a distance and blew into her. The effect of this action was that it passed through the mouth of Maryam 🌸 and thus, she was impregnated. As is well known, she later gave birth to ʿĪsā 🌸. Hence, Allāh 🌸 is highlighting that He created Ādam without a mother or father and to some extent, similiar is the case of ʿĪsā 🌸.

It can be ascertained through various verses and narrations that there were only three ways in which a human being could be created outside of the norm which requires both a mother and a father.

    i.   Without a mother and a father; the example of Ādam 🌸 substantiates this as he had no mother or father.

    ii.   Without a father; the example is of ʿĪsā 🌸 substantiates this.

    iii.   Without a mother; the example is of Ḥawwāʾ 🌸, the wife of Ādam 🌸. She was created from the ribs of Ādam 🌸 while he was sleeping in *Jannah*. Allāh 🌸 extracted one of his ribs and created Ḥawwāʾ 🌸 as is mentioned in the Qur'ān, *"...and from it created its match, and spread many men and women from the two."*[2]

ʿĪsā 🌸 was created in a special way and when he reached an age of maturity, he developed to become a mighty prophet of Allāh 🌸. Allāh 🌸 said:

"...and (Allāh 🌸 sent him as) a messenger to the Children of Isrāʾīl (who said to them), 'I have come to you with a sign from your Lord, that is, I make for you the form of a bird from clay, then I blow into it, and then it becomes a flying bird by the order of Allāh; and I cure the born-blind and the leper, and sometimes I bring the dead back to life by the will of Allāh.'"[3]

The words *'by the will of Allāh'* denote that his actions are not of his own accord but

---

[1] Al-Qur'ān 3:59

[2] Al-Qur'ān 4:1

[3] Sūrah Āle ʿImrān 3:49

rather, it happens by the command of Allāh 🌸. Thus, if he were to blow into a bird made from clay, it would not be able to soar unless Allāh 🌸 intended that for it. The word 'al-akmah' is in reference an individual who was born blind. So ʿĪsā 🌸 would recite the words, 'O the Living, O the All-Sustaining' and then and then blow into his hands before passing it over the blind individual. In some narrations he would recite 'O the Living, O the All-Sustaining' seven times. The term 'al-abraṣ' refers to an individual who is suffering from leprosy. ʿĪsā 🌸 would blow upon him and his leprosy would be cured.

Thereafter, ʿĪsā 🌸 mentions another of his qualities when he exclaims, "and sometimes I bring the dead back to life." A narration found within *Tafsīr al-Khāzin* indicates that ʿĪsā 🌸 ressurected seven dead people by the will of Allāh 🌸. It so happened that he and his disciples were passing by an area when ʿĪsā 🌸 said, "This grave is that of Sām ibn Nūḥ 🌸." The diciples requested, "O ʿĪsā, you are the Word of Allāh, could you ressurect him so we may converse with him?" Subsequently, ʿĪsā 🌸 supplicated to Allāh 🌸 and the deceased climbed out of his grave whilst in a shocked and terrified state. He enquired, "Has the Day of Standing commenced?! Is that why I am being taken out of my grave?!" ʿĪsā 🌸 replied, "No, it is because these people made a request to me. Hence, you have been brought back to life". They asked Sām ibn Nūḥ 🌸 as to his condition and he replied, "I have been dead for hundreds of years but I am still feeling the effect of the pangs of death within my body!"

Similarly, a young man had passed away and he was the lone child of his mother. While his body was being taken to the graveyard, his mother approached ʿĪsā 🌸 and implored him, "O ʿĪsā! He is my only child, I have nobody besides him, please, you must do something! Bring him back to life for me!" She pleaded with him and wept so bitterly that ʿĪsā 🌸 felt pity for her and so he supplicated to Allāh 🌸. He blew upon the young man who then stood up, took his shroud with him and returned home with his mother.

Such incidents are narrated about ʿĪsā 🌸 in various books of Qur'ānic exegesis under the commentary to the verse in contention.

The Prophets of Courage

Therefore, it is the Muslim belief that from among the prophets, one hundred and twenty four thousand were prophets, whereas three hundred and thirteen were also messengers. However, there are five from among them who are particularly distinguished. They are:

i. Nūḥ
ii. Ibrāhīm
iii. Mūsā
iv. ʿĪsā
v. Muḥammad ﷺ

They are hinted towards in the last verse of Sūrah al-Aḥqāf wherein Allāh says: *"O Muḥammad be patient, just as the Prophets of Courage were patient!"*[1]

The commentators of the Qur'ān are of the opinions that they are the prophets mentioned in Sūrah al-Aḥzāb wherein Allāh said:

> *"Remember O Muḥammad, the time when We took the Covenant from the prophets, we took for you and from Nūḥ, and from Ibrāhīm, and from Mūsā, and from ʿĪsā and we took a mighty and strong covenant from them!"*[2]

The Superiority of the Messenger of Allāh ﷺ

The oath that was taken from them was in relation to delivering the message of Allāh, fulfilling His Command and being steadfast - being prophets of courage. The aforementioned are the distinguished prophets in the eyes of Allāh. ʿAlī says, "Whichever prophet Allāh sent, he took an oath from him that if Muḥammad ﷺ was to appear during their life time, they would have to believe in him and assist him."

Similarly, Jābir relates that ʿUmar ibn al-Khaṭṭāb was once passing by a Jewish madrasa; they would also call their seminaries madrasas as well as they were proficient in Arabic. As ʿUmar was passing by, they were teaching the Torah to their children. Thus, ʿUmar sat down and began to listen to them. He liked some of the things that he had heard quite simply because it was good advice and so he asked, "May I borrow some of these papers?" They gave it to him and he proceeded to the company of the Messenger of Allāh ﷺ.

---

[1] Al-Qur'ān 46:35

[2] Al-Qur'ān 33:7

The Messenger of Allāh 🌸 was seated with some of his Companions 🌸 when ʿUmar 🌸 entered overjoyed. He approached the Messenger of Allāh 🌸 and said, "O Messenger of Allāh! I was passing by [the Jewish madrasa] and they were reading these scripts. There are some really good counsels in them! Can I read them to you?" He then began reading out of the paper. It is important to highlight that the Messenger of Allāh 🌸 was a very shy person. He would not rebuke anyone publicly but his displeasure would be evident as his face would turn red. Hence, when ʿUmar 🌸 read the contents of the paper, the Messenger of Allāh 🌸 became severely displeased but was withholding his disapproval. Abū Bakr as-Ṣiddīq 🌸, who was also present, saw the face of the Messenger of Allāh 🌸 and elbowed ʿUmar 🌸 to alert him. When ʿUmar 🌸 raised his gaze, he saw that the blessed face of the Messenger of Allāh 🌸 had turned red. ʿUmar immediately sat in the *tashahud* position, which denotes humility, and said, "O Messenger of Allāh! Forgive me! We are pleased with Allāh as our Lord, Islam as our religion and the Messenger of Allāh 🌸 as our Messenger!"

Thereafter, the Noble Prophet's 🌸 anger diminished and he exclaimed, "Why are you wandering hither and thither?! I have brought this religion to you which is as clear as broad daylight! Do not ask them of anything [i.e. for religious counsel], it might happen that they tell you something true and you reject it or that they may tell you something false and you might believe it. By He in whose Hand my soul lies, if Mūsā was alive today, he would have no choice but to follow me."

Once again, this narration complements the aforementioned Qurʾānic verse. Allāh 🌸 had taken an oath from Mūsā 🌸 that if the Noble Prophet 🌸 was to appear during his time, he would have had to follow the him 🌸.

Likewise, *al-ʿAllāmah* as-Suyūṭī 🌸 has related an incident pertaining to the superiority of the Messenger of Allāh 🌸 and his *Ummah*. When Mūsā 🌸 received the tablets from Allāh 🌸, he read the qualities of the *Ummah* of the Messenger of Allāh 🌸. He marvelled at it and was overjoyed by their characteristics. He beseeched his Lord and said "O Allāh! I read herein that there will be such people whose books will be preserved in their hearts. Grant me that *Ummah*." Allāh 🌸 replied, "No, this is the *Ummah* of Aḥmad [i.e. Muḥammad 🌸]." He went on to read several other characteristics and on every occasion, he said say, "Please grant me that *Ummah*!" However, on every occasion Allāh ﷻ replied, "No, this is the *Ummah* of Aḥmad."[1]

In some narrations he even requested that Allāh ﷻ makes him from this *Ummah*. Once again, Allāh ﷻ declined his request.

Soon after, ʿĪsā ﷺ also read the qualities of this *Ummah* and he supplicated, "O Allāh! I am not going to ask you for this *Ummah* but please include me within the *Ummah* of Muḥammad ﷺ." Allāh ﷻ accepted his prayer and took him high above the heavens, the account of which is well known. He will return before the end of time and defeat the Anti-Christ. Thereafter, he will guide the Muslims through the tribulation of Gog and Magog, and will remain in the world for some years. He will marry from which he will have two children and will then spend his final days in Madīnah al-Munawwarah . He will be buried alongside the Messenger of Allāh ﷺ, and the Two Shaykhs - Abū Bakr and ʿUmar ﷺ.[2]

In the chain of prophethood which started with Ādam ﷺ, the Messenger of Allāh ﷺ came as the final prophet. He was born in the year 571 AD and remained in this world for sixty three years. He was gifted with prophethood at the age of forty and resided in Makkah al-Mukarramah for thirteen years before migrating to Madīnah al-Munawwarah where he lived for ten years.

Publications on the Sīrah

It would take considerable time in explaining his blessed life and therefore, such a discussion would not be warranted at this time. For that, you will have to take some time out and find books pertaining to his blessed life. Make a habit of reading good books and if Allāh ﷻ wills, you will benefit. Undoubtedly, the more you read about Messenger of Allāḥ ﷺ, the closer you will feel to him. There are many good books about his blessed lifestyle available such as: '*Muḥammadur Rasūlullāh*' by Abū 'l-Ḥasan ʿAlī an-Nadwī ﷺ and '*The Sealed Nectar*' by Shaykh al-Mubārakpūrī ﷺ. Quite recently, a biography authoured by Tariq Ramadan was also published; it relates to the normal day to day life of the Messenger of Allāh ﷺ, and shows us how we can adapt our daily

---

[1] Al-Khaṣā'iṣ al-Kubrā

[2] Mishkat al-Masabīḥ

life and thereby follow his *Sunnah* in this era aswell. Other titles include: '*Sīrat al-Muṣṭafā*' by Maulānā Idrīs al-Khāndalwī and '*Sīrat al-Nu'mān*' by *al-ʿAllāmah* Shibli an-Nu'mānī.

The Characteristics of the Messenger of Allāh ﷺ

As we have now mentioned the Messenger of Allāh ﷺ, it would be ideal to mention his characteristics on the authority of those who were around him. His wife ʿĀ'ishah mentions many great attributes of his. Generally, a wife knows her husband the best and would notice the good and bad in him. She may be critical of something that is wrong and may want to hide whatever is good. However, the Messenger of Allāh ﷺ was a man of such sublime conduct that nobody could point a finger at him. His wives all spoke good about him. ʿĀ'ishah says, "The Messenger of Allāh ﷺ was not vulgar, nor would he pretend to be [vulgar]. He would not bellow in the market, nor would he repay evil with evil but rather, he would forgive and pardon."[1]

The statement '...was not vulgar' highlights that he would never swear at anyone and nor would he pretend to be a person who enjoys such language. He would never attempt to learn words of abuse in order to show others that he too can swear. Some individuals are not naturally foul mouthed but they are attracted to the manners adopted by others who do. As a result, they attempt to behave like them and thus use discourteous language. This is highlighted by the ḥadīth as vulgarity.

She then says that he would not bellow in the market places. To shout loud may be deemed suitable for a market place as many merchants are shouting and touting. Thus, such an environment may serve to influence a person but the statement of ʿĀ'ishah highlights that this was not the case in relation to the Messenger of Allāh ﷺ. He would maintain his dignity and honour at all times.

She concludes her description by saying, "...nor would he repay evil with evil but rather, he would forgive and pardon." If someone wronged him, he would never seek retribution. A desert dweller once came to him, grabbed hold of his upper garment and tugged at him. He fell into the chest of the desert dweller and his neck became bruised. The desert dweller, retorted in an extremely rude manner, "O Muḥammad!" He did not even call him by his title [i.e. the Messenger of Allāh]! Rather, he called him

[1] Ṣaḥīḥ al-Bukḥārī

by his name which was against the custom of the Companions. They would normally say, 'O Messenger of Allāh' or 'O Prophet of Allāh'. The desert dweller said, "O Muḥammad! Give me some wealth from the *Bait al-Māl* (Treasury)... not from your property or your father's property!" Do understand that this is an extremely rude remark. Any other person would have gone into a fit of rage but the Messenger of Allāh ﷺ turned to face him and then smiled. He replied, "Okay, I will specify [wealth] for you but give me my sheet back! You've pulled my cloak!" Thus, he took his sheet, covered himself and informed a companion, "Take him and give him whatever he wants from *Bait al-Māl.*"

In another ḥadīth, ʿĀ'ishah narrated, "The Messenger of Allāh ﷺ never hit anyone with his hand, not a woman, nor a servant..."[1] In another narration, it is further stated that he did not even hit a goat! The reason that this is mentioned is because it is common among shepherds to become angry when they are chasing after their flock. This can be quite frustrating and in this annoyance people tend to hit the sheep but ʿĀ'ishah highlights that the Messenger of Allāh ﷺ would not even hit a goat! At this point it is also important to note that the Messenger of Allāh ﷺ said in one ḥadīth, "There has not been a prophet except that he would tend to sheep. I used to look after them for the people of Makkah for a few *qīraṭ* [price]."[2] The reason for this is that looking after animals brings humility within a person. The sheep itself is a humble animal and when looking after it, it must be treated with gentleness, softness and kindness. It has small legs and if it is hit, there is a chance that it may be injured. Thus, Allāh made the prophets look after sheep so that they can develop gentleness and kindness within themselves.

Once Allāh asked Mūsā, 'O Mūsā! Do you know why I made you the One Who Converses [with Allāh] and why I spoke to you directly, unlike the other prophets?' Mūsā said, "No." Thereafter, Allāh replied, "O Mūsā! Once you were looking after a flock of sheep when one from among them ran away and you pursued it. It ran and ran, and you pursued it until the sheep became tired and so did you. You then took hold of the sheep, put her in your lap and while stroking her gently, you said, 'O sheep...why did you run? You tired yourself out and you tired me out too!' I was

---

[1] Ṣaḥīḥ Muslim

[2] Ṣaḥīḥ al-Bukhārī

observing you and I liked this action of yours so much that I made you One Who Converses [with Allāh].'

Thus, the Messenger of Allāh ﷺ never hit any of his wives, nor a servant or any goat. Anas ibn Mālik ؓ stated in one ḥadīth, "I served the Messenger of Allāh ﷺ for ten years, he never said '*uff*' to me. When I did something, he never said, 'Why did you do this?' And whenver I did not do something, he never said, 'Why did you leave this?'"[1]

The term '*uff*' is the lightest word by which one could show their disapproval of someone or something. For example, one may say, '*Uff!* what did you do?!"

The scholars are of the opinion that the statement, "When I did something, he never said, 'Why did you do this?' And whenver I did not do something, he never said, 'Why did you leave this?' " pertains to the service of Anas ؓ. If Anas ؓ did something wrong, for example, break a cup, the Messenger of Allāh ﷺ would never rebuke him or anyone else for that matter.

Anas ؓ was actually small boy of ten years when his mother brought him to the Messenger of Allāh ﷺ. She said, "O Messenger of Allāh ﷺ, Anas is my young child and he is very clever. I want him to stay in your service, he will stay with you, serve you and whatever needs you have, he will fulfill (them) for you. Please supplicate to Allāh ﷻ for him." The Messenger of Allāh ﷺ agreed, and thereafter Anas ؓ would live with his mother but during the day he would stay in the company of the Messenger of Allāh ﷺ and learn from him. When there would be work to attend to the Messenger of Allāh ﷺ would refer him and so he would go.

Once the Messenger of Allāh ﷺ instructed him, "Go Anas, go to so and so persons house." The young boy replied, "No O Messenger of Allāh, I am not in the mood, I am not going." The Messenger of Allāh ﷺ did not say anything. Anas ؓ stood up and left but as he departed, he had the intention to go as the Messenger of Allāh ﷺ instructed him to do so. However, he saw some boys playing and thus began to watch the game. After a while, the Messenger of Allāh ﷺ arrived and held him. He asked, "Anas, have you gone to the place that I told you to go?" He replied, "Yes! I am going O Messenger of Allāh!" He immediately left and completed the task.

ʿĀ'ishah ؓ further states, "Whenever the Messenger of Allāh ﷺ was given a choice between two matters, he would choose the one which is more easier, as long as it was

---

[1] Ibid

not a sin. If it was a sin, he would be the furthest away from it."[1] Whenever he was given a choice by Allāh ﷻ or by the people around him, Allāh ﷻ would inform him, 'O Muḥammad! You may do this or you could either do this.' Thereafter, the Messenger of Allāh ﷺ would look at which choice would be easier for his *Ummah* as he knew the *Ummah* was to follow him. Thus he would say that he did not want to put his *Ummah* in hardship but rather, he intended to make matters easy for them. He would choose the easier path for us as long as it was not a sin!

This ḥadīth is among those narrations that prove that the prophets are sinless. A prophet can never sin or disobey a command of Allāh ﷻ. A logical reason for this is because Allāh ﷻ sent prophets to be obeyed and followed. If a prophet was to sin, then his community would have to follow him in that also. Hence, Allāh ﷻ protected the prophets from disobedience, they never sinned or disobeyed Allāh ﷻ. They followed each and every command of His ﷻ.

In other narrations, ʿĀ'ishah ﷺ was asked, "What were the characteristics of the Messenger of Allāh ﷺ?" and she replied, "The Messenger of Allāh ﷺ was a human being from human beings. He would stay in the service of his family, he would mend his slippers, patch his clothes up, milk the goat and would do his own work himself. He would work in the house just as a normal person would work however, when it was time for prayer, he would depart for it."[2]

Furthermore, Anas ﷺ narrated, "The Prophet ﷺ was the most handsome among people. He was the most generous among people and he was the most courageous among people."[3]

He has also mentioned a famous incident that took place in Madīndah one night. The people of Madīnah were terrified by a loud noise. They slowly got out of their houses, congregated and proceeded to the mountain from behind which the noise occurred. They were suspecting that an army had come to attack Madīnah. However, as they had approached the mountain they saw the Messenger of Allāh ﷺ emerging from behind it on a horse which had no saddle and with a sword in his hand. He informed them that they should not worry, and that he has surveyed the area. Undoubtedly, he was the bravest among the people. He did not wait for anyone, he

[1] Ṣaḥīḥ Muslim

[2] Ibid

[3] Ibid

immediately rushed to that place and surveyed the area in order to protect his people, even if it be by himself.

Lastly, Anas ibn Mālik ؓ narrated, "The Prophet ﷺ woud visit the sick, follow the funeral procession, accept the invitation of a slave[1] and ride upon a donkey.[2] I saw him during the Battle of Khaibar [riding] upon a donkey whose reigns were made from the leaves of a palm tree [i.e. which would be extremely cheap]."[3]

Abū Saʿīd al-Khudrī ؓ also highlighted, "The Messenger of Allāh ﷺ was shyer than a virgin who has stayed behind curtains [throughout her entire life]. When he disliked something, we could tell by his face."[4] Contextually, this is amazing; one must ask to how much modesty would a young girl of that era have? Regardless, the Messenger of Allāh ﷺ would be even more modest than her! The Companions ؓ have mentioned, "His face would change..." it would turn red and they would know that something has brought him displeasure. Thus, they would apologise.

ʿAbd Allāh ibn Abī ʿAwfā ؓ said, "The Messenger of Allāh would frequently be engaged in the rememberance of Allāh. He would talk less about futile things and would prolong his prayer. He would shorten his [Friday] sermon."[5]

Likewise, Abū Saʿīd al-Khudrī ؓ said, "Sometimes he would be in a sitting and he would be engaged in *dhikr* and *tasbīḥ*. We could count him saying '*Astagfirullāh*' one hundred times." His heart would be attached to Allāh ﷻ.

The statement, "He would shorten his [Friday] sermon" indicates that on Friday, he would not stand up on the pulpit for a lengthy period of time. His sermons would bear brevity but meaning. When he would stand up at night for prayer, he would lengthen his prayer. He would get up for *taḥajjud* prayer and would continue to pray throughout most of the night. Despite having his beautiful young wife ʿĀ'ishah ؓ by his side, he would still get up and exclaim, "O ʿĀ'ishah, give me permission so that I may worship my Lord ﷻ." She would reply, "O Messenger of Allāh! Who am I to stop you?"

---

[1] A servant or slave would have only earned a meagre income and so if he invited people for food, he would have no choice but to cook a modest meal. Nevertheless, the Messenger of Allāh ﷺ would not refuse the invitation, regardless of whether it was from a slave or not.

[2] He would not ask for flashy horses to ride but he would use whatever was available.

[3] Ṣaḥīḥ Muslim

[4] Ibid

[5] Sunan an-Nasa'ī

ʿĀ'ishah ؓ stated, "Once I woke up and the Messenger of Allāh ﷺ was not by my side. The thought came to me that perhaps he had gone to one of his other wives. Thus, I started searching for him when suddenly, I found him in prostration saying, "O Allāh, I seek refuge in Your pardon from Your punishment and refuge in Your pleasure from Your anger. I seek refuge in You [due to the fact that] I cannot praise You as You deserve to be praised! You are as You have praised Yourself." ʿĀ'ishah ؓ said, "May my mother and father be sacrificed for you. You are in one condition and I am in another."[1]

This does not mean that he was not a family man; he was incredibly family orientated. He would behave joyfully in his house, fulfill the needs of his family, and take care of their needs. When sifting through narrations, it is evident that he was an incredibly caring and affectionate husband. He was once with ʿĀ'ishah ؓ and the Companions ؓ were also with him; he instructed the Companions ؓ to proceed ahead. When they were at a distance, he turned to ʿĀ'ishah ؓ and said, "ʿĀ'ishah ؓ! Let's race!" It just so happened that ʿĀ'ishah ؓ won the race and the Messenger of Allāh ﷺ was left behind. However, after sometime, the same incident reoccurred. This time however, the Messenger of Allāh ﷺ won and so he teased, "I have taken my revenge!" This is just a small example of the great manner in which he treated his wives. Truly, he was a genuinely nice person.

To proceed, we are in attendance in order to talk about the superiority of the Messenger ﷺ as is highlighted by the title of the book. After this brief introduction, it is imperative for the sake of our discourse to now understand who the most distinguished messengers are and in which way Allāh ﷻ gave virtues to each of them. He gave them special attributes, virtues, scriptures, and miracles. The Messenger of Allāh ﷺ was gifted with many special miracles which we will discuss in the next session if Allāh ﷻ wills. As yet, we have introduced the Messenger of Allāh ﷺ to our discussion by mentioning some of his magnificient characteristics.

~ End of Session One ~

---

[1] Ibid

Session Two

A Brief Biography of Shaykh ʿIzz ad-Dīn ibn ʿAbd al-Salām 🌸

The author of this book is *al-Imām* ʿIzz ad-Dīn ibn ʿAbd al-Salām 🌸 and it has been translated from Arabic into English by Sister Aishah Bewley. *Al-Imām* ʿIzz ad-Dīn ibn ʿAbd al-Salām 🌸 was born in the year 577 AH corresponding to 1181 AD. He was a follower of the Shāfiʿī school of thought and is considered by many from among the greatest scholars of his time. Infact, in some rulings he was like a *mujtahid* in that he had issued legal verdicts regarding advances that had developed during his lifetime. Thus, he possessed a very high rank within the Muslim community.

He was educated in Damascus, Syria, where he was born. Thereafter, he travelled to Baghdad, Iraq which was considered to be one of the greatest centres of learning at the time. After he had quenched his thirst for knowledge, he returned to Damascus, where he was made the Imam of the Ummayad Mosque. It was at this mosque where he would deliver the Friday sermon and regular lectures. *Al-Imām* al-Ghazālī 🌸, whose full name is Abū Ḥāmid Muḥammad ibn Muḥammad ibn Muḥammad al- Ghazālī 🌸, passed away in the year 555 AH whereas ʿIzz ad-Dīn ibn ʿAbd al-Salām 🌸 was born in the year 571 AH. This indicates that there is not much of a gap between them; perhaps there was a gap of fifty years before ʿIzz ad-Dīn ibn ʿAbd al-Salām 🌸 replaced al-Ghazālī 🌸 as a Shāfiʿī authority.

ʿIzz ad-Dīn ibn ʿAbd al-Salām 🌸 was also known for the great courage that he would exhibit. He was outspoken in his views and would not be intimidated by the rulers as many others were. His honest nature and integrity prevented him from distorting the verses of the Qurʾān or ḥadīth in order to appease the rulers of the time – a theme which was bitterly prevalent among them. Once, it just so happened that the rulers acted indecently by giving land to the enemies of the time. ʿIzz ad-Dīn ibn ʿAbd al-Salām 🌸 spoke out and was subsequently imprisoned as a result.

It was for this reason he (ʿIzz ad-Dīn 🌸) was given the title '*Sultān al-ʿUlamā*' (the Leader of Scholars) because he did not desist in speaking the truth and none could equal his efforts. The fact that an-Nawawī 🌸 has narrated the opinions of ʿIzz ad-Dīn

🐝 is his commentary of Ṣaḥīḥ Muslim is indicative of the latter's acceptance and rank among the scholars.

When he was released from prison, he realised that it was no longer suitable to stay in Damascus and so he migrated to Cairo, Egypt where he received a warm welcome. The ruler of Egypt venerated him and held him in high esteem; consequently, ʿIzz ad-Dīn 🐝 was made an authority in one of Egypt's highest courts. Thus, he spent the remainder of his life there and also found a place where he could speak openly and author books. Later on in his life, he authored many books such as 'Qawāiʾd al-Aḥkām fī Masāliḥ al-Anām'.

As mentioned previously, ʿIzz ad-Dīn ibn ʿAbd al-Salām 🐝 would monitor key developments within the Muslim community. He would advise that one must analyse the Qurʾān and ḥadīth in relation to the necessities of the time. ʿUmar ibn ʿAbd al-ʿAzīz 🐝 (d. 101 AH) once said, "[At times], legal verdicts are issued to the public in response to the impiety that they have facilitated."

For example, some ḥadīth advise one to stand up from their seat when a venerated person enters a room. In one narration, the Messenger of Allāh 🌸 said, "Stand up for your leader." However, another narration highlights that the Messenger of Allāh 🌸 said, "Do not stand in the manner the non Arabs stand." It is for this reason that ʿUmar ibn ʿAbd al-ʿAzīz 🐝 articulated that a jurist has to give a verdict according to the need of the time. It so happened that during the time of ʿIzz ad-Dīn ibn Jamāʿah 🐝 (one of the contemporaries of ʿIzz ad-Dīn ibn ʿAbd al-Salām 🐝), people disputed regarding this ruling, to the extent that some said it was compulsory whilst others maintained that it was forbidden. The scholars attempted to justify their views by the two conflicting ḥadīth but were not able to reconcile. Thus, ʿIzz ad-Dīn ibn Jamāʿah 🐝 advised, "Do not simply give [legal] verdicts based upon the words of the ḥadīth but take everything into full context, including societal norms." Such are our times that if we do not stand up for individuals, they develop malice within their hearts! In various ḥadīth, it is mentioned, "Do not be jealous of one another, do not hold malice against one another, do not plot behind the backs of one another!" Therefore, in order to maintain harmony, it would be advisable to stand up for a venerated individual in respect of them. From this we learn that at times, we have to adapt with societal norms and such principles are mentioned in ʿIzz ad-Dīn ibn ʿAbd al-Salām's 🐝 book

Qawāi'd al-Aḥkām fī Masāliḥ al-Anām. He eventually passed away in the year 666 AH corresponding to 1262 AD.

We will now commence our study of the book:

The Lineage of the Messenger of Allāh ﷺ

بسم الله الرحمن الرحيم

In the Name of Allāh, the All-Merciful, Most Merciful. O Allāh, bless our master Muḥammad and his family and grant him peace, and help and grant ease, and perfect [this book]. Praise belongs to Allāh Who created mankind and favoured him with the two smallest matters, the heart and the tongue. I praise Him for the clear expression He taught, and I give thanks for the kindness He showed. I testify that there is no god but Allāh alone without a partner, a testimony by which I hope to attain safety, and I testify that Muḥammad is His Messenger, the one chosen from amongst the descendants of ʿAdnān.

ʿAdnān is from among the descendants of Ibrāhīm ﷺ, the great ancestor of the Messenger of Allāh ﷺ. His lineage goes through to Maʿād ibn ʿAdnān who lived during the time of ʿĪsā ﷺ when he was a prophet in Jerusalem. During this time, ʿAdnān was residing in Makkah al-Mukarramah. The following is the lineage of the Noble Prophet ﷺ: *Muḥammad ibn ʿAbd Allāh ibn ʿAbd al-Muṭṭalib ibn Ḥāshim ibn ʿAbd Munāf ibn Quṣai ibn Kilāb ibn Murrah ibn Kaʿb ibn Lu'ayy ibn Ghālib ibn Fihr ibn Mālik ibn an-Naḍr ibn Kinānah ibn Khuzaimah ibn Mudrikah ibn Ilyās ibn Muḍr ibn Nizār ibn Maʿād ibn ʿAdnān.*

The Qur'ān – A Great Miracle

So, the one chosen from amongst the descendants of ʿAdnān, and helped with patent miracles, the Qur'ān, dazzling lights, and a proof, who was preferred over all created things including the angels, men and *jinn*, may the blessings of Allāh be upon him as long as equals are in harmony and opposites in discord.

The words **'dazzling lights, and a proof'** are descriptions by which the author is describing the Qur'ān. The Qur'ān truly is a dazzling light. I recently came across a book entitled, *'Why Islām is Our Choice'* in which the accounts of various reverts who accepted Islām have been narrated. I read the story of one individual whose words had touched me. To paraphrase, they had said:

> *"I was in search of a religion and I had studied many. When I came upon Islam, I started to read the Qur'ān and the only thing I can say is that the example of this (Qur'ān) is like that of a large building with many rooms. If you open the door of every room, you may find some light in that room. Then picture yourself going around until suddenly you come to a massive hall, and in that hall you open another door. As soon as you open the door, the light is so dazzling that it stuns your eyes. This is the example of the books that I have read from other religions. There is some light within the books but the big room that I entered is the room of the Qur'ān. As soon as you open the doors of the room of the Qur'ān, there is so much light that your eyes are dazzled and you have to compose yourself before you proceed. You cannot realise the value of the Qur'ān unless you have been deprived of it beforehand."*

'Izz ad-Dīn ibn 'Abd al-Salām 🕌 also describes the Qur'ān as a **'proof'**. It bears testament to the fact that the Messenger of Allāh 🕌 truly is a prophet. As mentioned previously, the Messenger of Allāh 🕌 was gifted with many, many miracles as were the prophets before him. 'Īsā 🕌 came with the miracle of curing the sick and bringing dead back to life, Ibrāhīm 🕌 was thrown into the fire and came out alive and the likes of Mūsā 🕌 would throw down a staff only for it to morph into a snake. He would also place his hand under his armpit and it would begin to shine when he would remove it. Such was its radiance that it was possible for him to walk throughout the darkness of night. When he would place his hand under his armpit, it would once again return to its original state. The Messenger of Allāh's 🕌 miracles are of two types:

i. Those that occurred during his lifetime. For example, the gushing of water from his fingers when he had put his hands into a bowl of water, the splitting of the moon when pointed his finger towards it and so on. These were miracles which were observed by the naked eye. The Companions 🕌 were accustomed to seeing such miracles on a regular basis.

ii. Those that are abstract such as spirituality.

The greatest miracle given to the Messenger of Allāh 🕌 from Allāh 🕌 is the Qur'ān

– the Living Miracle. Maulānā Rūm mentions that when Firʿaun brought the magicians to confront Mūsā, they were perplexed. Two of them went to their aged father who was bed ridden and sought his consultation regarding Mūsā. They asked their father, "Is he truly a prophet of Allāh? Is his work a miracle or is he a sorcerer?" Their father replied, "Do as I am about to tell you; approach Mūsā whilst he is asleep and seek to steal his staff. If you succeed, break it into two pieces. If it breaks then this indicates that he is a magician. However, if you fail in this endeavour it means that he is not a magician but a messenger of God and indeed what happens to that staff is a miracle!" Thus, they remained in search of Mūsā until they eventually found him sleeping under a tree. The two magicians tip-toed towards him and as they approached, the staff transformed into a snake and jumped up at them! They fled and realised that the transformation was not sorcery as magic can only work when the magician is focused on the illusion at hand. In this case, his staff turned into a snake whilst he was asleep! Hence, they realised that it was not enchantment but a miracle of Allāh.

After narrating this incident, Maulānā Rūm writes, "O reader of my book! Mūsā's miracle was with him for as long as he remained in this world. When he left, his miracle also left with him. The staff did not turn into a snake thereafter! However, Muḥammad ﷺ – the Messenger of Allāh, your Prophet, his biggest miracle was the Qur'ān which is alive and evident with us even today! This miracle is alive even though Muḥammad ﷺ has passed away. Therefore, it is your responsibility to read the Qur'ān, witness the miracle of Messenger of Allāh ﷺ and thereafter accept him as the prophet of Allāh."

"We favoured some of these Messengers over others..."

To proceed; I requested my father ʿIzz ad-Dīn ibn ʿAbd al-Salām to dictate to me something about how the Prophet ﷺ is preferred over all men, and he replied instantly and without restraint saying:

Allāh, exalted is He, says to our Prophet Muḥammad ﷺ out of generosity to him and apprising us of his worth to Him: *"Allāh has sent down the Book and Wisdom on*

***you and taught you what you did not know. Allāh's favour to you is indeed immense*"[1] Allāh, exalted is He, has favoured some messengers over others, He says, "*We favoured some of these Messengers over others.* Allāh *spoke directly to some of them and raised up some of them in rank.*"[2]**

The commentators of the Qur'ān have mentioned a variety of points pertaining to this verse. The statement, "...among them there are those with whom Allāh conversed and spoke directly..." is a reference to Mūsā ﷺ. Likewise, the phrase, "...we gave ʿĪsā son of Maryam clear proofs..." is a direct mention of ʿĪsā ﷺ. However, in between Allāh ﷻ has stated, "And there are some whose ranks Allāh raised." The reference is to Muḥammad ﷺ who was chosen above all others.

I was reading a delightful book called, '*Naḍrah an-Naʿīm*' by Shaykh Ṣāliḥ ibn Ḥumaid who is currently serving as one of the imams of Masjid al-Ḥarām, Makkah. He regularly used to lead Fajr prayer and is now among the consultation council. The book mentioned above focuses upon the biography of the Messenger of Allāh ﷺ. It spans over eight large volumes wherein he discusses many matters linked to the Noble Prophet ﷺ. When discussing the 'Virtues of the Messenger ﷺ', he divides it into four categories:

i. The special virtues given to Messenger of Allāh ﷺ in this world.
ii. The special virtues given to the Messenger of Allāh ﷺ in the hereafter.
iii. The virtues given to his *Ummah* and his followers in this world.
iv. The virtues given to his *Ummah* and his followers in the hereafter.

He then details each attribute with examples. A brief summary is as follows:

The Special Virtues Given to the Messenger of Allāh ﷺ in this World

1. Allāh ﷻ took an oath from the other prophets regarding the Messenger of Allāh ﷺ. If he was to appear during their lifetime they would have to follow him. For example, if Mūsā ﷺ was alive and the Noble Prophet ﷺ was to enter into this world, the former would have to believe in him and assist him. That is why the Messenger of Allāh ﷺ in one ḥadīth, "If Mūsā was alive, he would have no choice but to follow me." Allāh ﷻ mentions this oath in Sūrah Āle ʿImrān wherein He

[1] Al-Qur'ān 4:113

[2] Al-Qur'ān 2:253

said:

"When Allāh made the prophets enter into a covenant (saying): 'If I give you a book and wisdom, then comes to you a messenger verifying what is with you, you shall have to believe in him, and you shall have to support him.' He said, 'Do you affirm and accept my covenant in this respect?' They said, 'We affirm.' He said, 'Then, bear witness, and I am with you among the witnesses.' "[1]

2. His call was to the entirety of humanity and he was in himself a universal prophet. His call was even to the *jinn* as Allāh ﷻ mentions:

"And when we directed a group of jinn to you, they came listening to the Qur'ān. When they arrived they said, 'keep quiet!' when they returned to their people as warners to them. They said, 'O our people! We have heard a book which was sent down after Mūsa which confirms that which was before it. It guides to the truth and to the straight path! O our people! Respond to the caller of Allāh and believe in him. Allāh will forgive for you some of your sins and He will protect you from a painful punishment."[2]

This verse encapsulates the dialogue which took place between the *jinn* which has been documented in Sūrah al-Aḥqāf. It proves that the Messenger of Allāh ﷺ was also sent to the *jinn* as well and it is also important to note that many among the *jinn* had accepted Islām upon his hands.

Badr ad-Dīn ash-Shiblī has mentioned in '*Ākām al-Marjān fī Aḥkām al-Jān*' that the Messenger of Allāh ﷺ met with the *jinn* approximately six to seven times. Three or four of these meetings occurred in Makkah al-Mukarramah and three meetings took place in Madīnah. There were occasions when the Noble Prophet ﷺ proceeded to the mountains and outskirts of Madīnah in order to educate the *jinn*. Abū Ḍharr al-Ghifārī ؓ had accompanied him and at another time, ʿAbd Allāh ibn Masʿūd ؓ was with him. The *jinn* would thereafter accept Islām upon the blessed hands of the Messenger of Allāh ﷺ.

At this juncture, an astonishing incident comes to mind. It is known that if a *jinn* met the Messenger of Allāh ﷺ, it would be classed as a companion. However, a

---

[1] Al-Qur'ān 3:81

[2] Al-Qur'ān 46:29-31

question arises, what if a person then met that *jinn*? Would he be classed as a *tābiʿī*?[1] This incident occurred in the time of Shah Walī Allāh ad-Dehlawī or perhaps his father's era.

A scholar was studying his books when suddenly, a snake appeared before him. He immediately stood up, beat it with a stick and consequently killed it. The next day, someone came to collect him and said, "A case has been made against you, you have to come to court with us!"

It would be useful to mention at this point that the scholars of the past used to make the supplication, "May Allāh protect us from two places: the hospital and the courtroom." We should also make this supplication as the elders from our *Ummah* had a lot of wisdom!

The scholar replied, "What?! I haven't done anything wrong! Why should I go to the court?" However, the man insisted and they departed. As they travelled, the scholar noticed that the person was taking him out of the city of Delhi. He immediately asked him, "The court should be in the town centre! Why have you taken me outside the city for?" The man replied, "No, the court is elsewhere." They kept walking until they came to a place where there were lots of trees, bushes and water. There, the scholar noticed a huge gathering and that a funeral was taking place. He was ushered in front of the judge and it was then that he realised from the physical appearance that they were a group of *jinn*. He enquired, "What have I done wrong?" They responded, "There is a case against you as you have killed one of our folks." He maintained that he hadn't killed anyone but they informed him, "Last night you sat down to read, a snake appeared which was in reality a *jinn*. You killed it!"

The scholar began to plead his innocence and said, "I did not know that it was a *jinn*! I killed it thinking it to be a snake!" They said, "Whatever the case, you have killed him and you will be killed in retaliation. *Qiṣāṣ* will be exacted upon you." He was left dumbfounded and there was nothing else to say. In the meantime, there was a lot of bickering among the *jinn* when suddenly, an elderly *jinn* emerged and intervened. He said, "I have heard the Messenger of Allāh ﷺ saying, 'Whomsoever took the form of a certain community of people and was killed because of that, then his blood is void

[1] The Tābi'ūn were the generation of Muslims who were born after the Noble Prophet's ﷺ era but were contemporaries of the Companions.

[i.e. retaliation should not be exacted].' "[1]

After enquiring further, the judge then dismissed the case and the scholar was free to go. When he returned, he was extremely chuffed and said to people, "I am a *tābiʿī* as I met a Companion!" Whilst narrating this story, Shah Walī Allāh ad-Dehlawī states, "If he met a companion and became a *tābiʿī* then I am *tābiʿ* at-*tābiʿīn*[2] because I met him!"

After narrating this incident, my honourable teacher, Shaykh Yūnus (may Allāh protect him) mentioned, "One cannot become a *tābiʿī* or a *tābiʿ* at-*tābiʿīn* because of this incident but he may be able to gain virtue for narrating from a *jinn* who related this ḥadīth. This is because *tābiʿī* or a *tābiʿ* at-*tābiʿīn* is special terminology for a person who met a companion during their lifetime. It is defined as a special group or generation of people. As the scholar in discussion is not from them, he would not be classed as a *tābiʿī*. Nevertheless, he would have gained some virtue as a result of meeting that *jinn*."

3. He is the final prophet of Allāh; Allāh said to him, *"He is the Messenger of Allāh and the Seal of the prophets."*[3] In one ḥadīth the Messenger of Allāh ﷺ has said, "I am the seal of the prophets. There is no [new] prophet after me."[4] Likewise, the Messenger of Allāh ﷺ also said, "I came and I finished [the succession] the prophets."[5]

4. He was guiding mercy. Allāh said, *"We have not sent you but as a mercy for the whole universe."*[6] He was a very compassionate, merciful person and brought the message of peace to the universe.

5. He was a source of safety for his Companions during his lifetime. He said, "The stars are a [source of] security for the skies; when they start to fade[upon the blowing of the Trumpet], the sky will be overcome by whatever is promised to it. I am a [source of] security for my Companions; when I go, my Companions will be confronted with whatever is promised to them. [Finally] my Companions are a

---

[1] من تزيا بزي قوم فقتل فرمه هدر

[2] The generation that came after the Tābiʿūn.

[3] Al-Qur'ān 33:40

[4] Sunan at-Tirmidhī

[5] Ṣaḥīḥ Muslim

[6] Al-Qur'ān 21:107

[source of] security for my *Ummah*. When they go, my *Ummah* will have to face whatever is destined for them."[1]

6. Allāh ﷻ took an oath upon the life of the Messenger of Allāh ﷺ when He said, *"By your life! Surely, they are in their intoxication, wondering aimlessly!"*[2] Such an oath has never been made upon the life of any other prophet.

7. Allāh ﷻ called out to him through his attributes and not his name. ʿIzz ad-Dīn ibn ʿAbd al-Salām has also mentioned this in his book. Allāh ﷻ has addressed other prophets by their names. For example, He said, 'O Ādam', 'O ʿĪsā', 'O Mūsā' but He never said, 'O Muḥammad'. Rather, He addressed him and said, 'O Messenger', 'O Prophet', 'O Messenger', 'O Enshrouded One', 'O Cloaked One' and so on. This is the high esteem in which Allāh ﷻ holds the Messenger of Allāh ﷺ.

As we are discussing the names of the Messenger of Allāh ﷺ, it is good to note that he is mentioned four times in the Qur'ān by his name. They are:

i. *"Muḥammad is but a messenger."*[3]

ii. *"Muḥammad is not a father of any of your men, but he is a messenger of Allāh and the last of the prophets."*[4]

iii. *"And those who believed and did righteous deeds and believed in that which is revealed to Muḥammad..."*[5]

iv. *"Muḥammad is the messenger of Allāh."*[6]

The Messenger of Allāh ﷺ is also mentioned by his name, 'Aḥmad' in Sūrah aṣ-Ṣaff Allāḥ ﷻ says:

> *"(Remember) when ʿĪsā the son of Maryam said said, 'O children of Isrā'īl, I am a messenger of Allāh sent towards you, confirming the Torah that is (sent down) before me, and giving you the good news of a messenger who will come after me, whose name will be Aḥmad.'"*[7]

Those who are sceptics attempt to create confusion over this verse by objecting,

---

[1] Ṣaḥīḥ Muslim

[2] Al-Qur'ān 15:72

[3] Al-Qur'ān 3:145

[4] Al-Qur'ān 33:40

[5] Al-Qur'ān 47:2

[6] Al-Qur'ān 48:29

[7] Al-Qur'ān 61:6

"If his name is Muḥammad, why did ʿIsā ﷺ refer to him as Aḥmad?' The answer is simple; at times, the mother's family would like one name and the father's side would like another name and as the child grows up, one of his names is used more than the other and thus he becomes famous by it. This is what happened to the Messenger of Allāh ﷺ; his mother chose the name Aḥmad and his grandfather chose the name Muḥammad and as he grew up, he became known by Muḥammad. Similarly, the Messenger of Allāh ﷺ has mentioned in one ḥadīth, "I have several names. I am Muḥammad. I am Aḥmad..." He then went onto say, "I am al-Māḥī with whom Allāh wipes out disbelief. I am al-Ḥāshir behind whom people will be gathered [on the Day of Standing]. I am al-ʿĀqib after whom there will be no prophet."[1]

8. Allāh ﷻ forbade the believers from calling him by his name. Allāh ﷻ commanded the believers not to address him by his name but to address him by his titles. He said in Sūrah an-Nūr: *"Do not make your call to the Messenger as you call one another."*[2]

9. He was gifted with *jawāmiʿ al-kalim.* This is the ability to articulate precise and succinct speech which bear oceans of meaning in them.

10. He was bestowed with an awe-inspiring quality to the extent that wherever he would be, people would be in awe of him and be inspired by his presence.

ʿAbd Allāh ibn ʿAbbas ؓ used to say that many disbelievers were at a distance of one month but they were too scared to confront Messenger of Allāh ﷺ. They felt intimidated to speak negatively about him. Even the likes of Ceasar, who was such a mighty ruler, who had the entire Roman Empire under his control was extra cautious of Messenger of Allāh ﷺ. When the letter of Messenger of Allāh ﷺ was read out in his court, which was full of his parliamentarians, he was struck by awe and said, "This person is a true prophet! If I was at his side, I would serve him, wash his feet and I would do his service... If what you have said is true, he will be the owner of that land which is under my chair [i.e. his will rule the lands which are under my sovereignty]."[3]

Al-Hāfiẓ ibn Hajar ؒ said, "The attribute of awe was given to Messenger of Allāh ﷺ to such an extent that if he was facing an army alone, his awe-inspiring quality would be enough to strike fear into the enemy." If we analyse the Battle of Ḥunain,

---

[1] Ṣaḥīḥ al-Bukhārī & Ṣaḥīḥ Muslim

[2] Al-Qur'ān 24:63

[3] Ṣaḥīḥ al-Bukḥārī

the Messenger of Allāh ﷺ was with the army when the tribe of Hawāzin made a sudden attack. Those who were at the forefront of the Muslim army began to flee due to the plethora of arrows that were being fired at them. The enemy then began to advance from the front and the Muslims fled. At this stage, Messenger of Allāh ﷺ was advancing and with him were only a group of a hundred people. He kept moving forward saying, "I am the Messenger, not a liar. I am the son of Ibn ʿAbd al-Muṭṭalib."

He did this to the extent that at one point, he would only have the likes of Abū Sufyān ibn al-Hārithah and ʿAbbās ibn al-Muṭṭalib on either side of him. Despite very little assistance, he continued to proceed. He would take some soil and as he threw it, he would say, "May these faces become disfigured!" As a result, their sight was obscured and they began to flee. The Muslim army marched forward and Allāh gave them victory.

11. The Messenger of Allāh ﷺ was given the keys to the treasures of the earth and he passed it onto the Companions. Wherever they went, they conquered and gained much affluence.

12. The mistakes of the Messenger of Allāh ﷺ were pardoned; any minor errors due to being human were forgiven in advance.

13. The Messenger of Allāh ﷺ was granted a Book that is to remain till the Day of Standing and will not be distorted.

14. The Messenger of Allāh ﷺ was gifted with *al-Isrā* and *al-Miʿrāj* (The Night Journey).

15. The blessed chest of the Messenger of Allāh ﷺ was opened, his heart was taken out, cleansed with *Zam Zam* and filled with belief and wisdom. It was then put back into its original place and the chest was sewn back together. This was exclusive to Messenger of Allāh ﷺ and no such incident took place with any prophet before him.

The Special Virtues Given to the Messenger of Allāh ﷺ in the Hereafter

1. The Messenger of Allāh ﷺ has been granted a special rank in Jannah which is not suitable for any other person apart from him.

2. In the hereafter, the Messenger of Allāh ﷺ will be gifted with the Station of Praise; this is a special position where everybody will praise him. Whoever sees him will praise him, the other prophets will also praise him.

3. The Messenger of Allāh ﷺ will be gifted with the Great Intercession. When everyone will be resurrected, they will proceed to the plain of Resurrection. They will be stopped there and will want the Reckoning to start. Years will have passed by and no one will be able to request Allāh ﷻ to commence the proceedings. Hence, people will seek out the prophets and urge them to intercede. All will refuse this request until they finally come to Messenger of Allāh ﷺ who will say, "I am to do this." He will fall prostrate before Allāh ﷻ in which he will praise Him to such an extent that Allāh ﷻ will say "O Muḥammad! Raise your head, say and you will be heard! Ask and you will be given. Intercede, your intercession will be accepted."

Thereafter, the Noble Prophet ﷺ will raise his head and request for the Reckoning to begin which will then commence.

Likewise, on the Day of Standing, he will be gifted with the Fountain of al-Kawthar. People will come to him thirsty and he will offer them sweet water with his own hands. They will drink from the special fountain before the Reckoning starts and will not feel thirsty after that. This will be specially gifted to him in the hereafter as mentioned in the authentic narrations.

The Special Virtues Given to His Ummah in this World

1.His *Ummah* have been made the Best of Nations. In one verse, Allāh ﷻ says, "*You are the best Ummah ever raised for mankind. You bid the fair and forbid the unfair, and you believe in Allāh.*"[1]

Likewise, the Messenger of Allāh ﷺ, "You will be completing seventy nations, you are the best of them and the most honoured in the Sight of Allāh."[2]

Similarly, al-Būsīrī ﷺ wrote in his famous poem, "When Allāh addressed our Messenger as the most noble amongst the messengers, we were also [by default] addressed as the most noble amongst the nations."

2.The acquisition of war booty was permitted for this *Ummah* whereas it had been prohibited for other nations.

3.It is permissible for this *Ummah* to offer their prayers anywhere on earth.

[1] Al-Qur'ān 3:110

[2] Sunan at-Tirmidhī

Previous nations had to go to their places of worship to pray but this *Ummah* can pray wherever they are whether it be on a journey, at an airport or at a station.

4.The earth was made a source of purification for this *Ummah.* If we cannot acquire water, we may do *tayammum* as opposed to ablution and bathing.

5.The *Ummah* has been gifted with the day of Friday (al-Jummᶜuah). The best of days is the day of Friday due to the countless blessings it possesses. Allāh ﷻ awarded it to this *Ummah.*

6.Mistakes committed due to forgetfulness have been forgiven. If we make a mistake, it is forgiven for us whereas the previous nations would be held to account for their errors and forgetfulness. The Messenger of Allāh ﷺ said, "The [reckoning of] mistakes and forgetfulness have been withdrawn from my *Ummah* along with things that they have been coerced into doing."[1]

7.The *Ummah* has been protected from complete annihilation. - Among the previous nations, there were some who were annihilated in their entirety. For example, the nations of Nūḥ, Hūd, Ṣāliḥ, Shuᶜaib and Lūṭ ﷺ all suffered a horrific end. However, the Messenger of Allāh ﷺ supplicated for the protection of his *Ummah* and as a result, it will be protected from total annihilation till the Day of Standing.

8.The Messenger of Allāh ﷺ supplicated to Allāh ﷻ so that his *Ummah* do not unite upon error and deviance. Even though there might be individuals among them who will try to mislead others, there will always be people who will combat false ideas and guide people towards the right path.

The Special Virtues Given to His Ummah in the Hereafter

1. The *Ummah* will be the most among the inhabitants of *Jannah* and this will come to light on the Day of Qiyāmah. The Messenger of Allāh ﷺ said, "When the reckoning will be done, people will come to the Bridge. The rows of people going into *Jannah* will be formed and there will one hundred and twenty rows. Eighty of those will be of my *Ummah* and forty will belong to other nations."

This is a brief list of what Shaykh Ṣaliḥ ibn Ḥumaid has mentioned in his book.

[1] Sunan ibn Mājah

We will now move on to the specialities of the Messenger of Allāh ﷺ as mentioned by ʿIzz ad-Dīn ibn ʿAbd al-Salām.

The Master of Mankind

1. **He is the master of all mankind. He ﷺ said, "I am the leader of the Children of Ādam and this is no boast." 'The Master' is whoever is characterised by sublime attributes and luminous qualities of character. This shows us that he is better than them [i.e. other prophets] in both abodes. As for in this world, it is because he is characterised by tremendous qualities of character. As for the Next World, it is because repayment is arranged according to one's qualities and character. Since he is better than them in this world in virtues and attributes, he is better than them in the Next world in his ranks and degrees. He ﷺ said, "I am the master of the children of Ādam, and it is no boast" to inform his community about his position in respect to his Lord – Mighty and Exalted is He! As mentioning one's virtues is usually done out of pride, the Prophet ﷺ meant to dispel the illusion of any ignorant person, who might assume that he stated it merely in order to boast, by saying, "It is not boast."**

The ḥadīth, "I am the master of the children of Ādam and it is no boast" is not a statement of pride but rather, it is a proclamation which the Messenger of Allāh ﷺ had been ordered to make by Allāh. He says, "As for the blessings of your Lord, narrate them [i.e. relate them to the people]."[1]

In the passage above, Shaykh ʿIzz ad-Dīn ibn ʿAbd al-Salām highlights that the Messenger of Allāh ﷺ was gifted with tremendous qualities and characteristics. Everything pertaining to his mannerisms was of a sublime nature it to such an extent that Allāh made mention of it in the opening verses of Sūrah al-Qalam. He said:

[1] Al-Qur'ān 93:11

"Nūn. By the pen and what people note down. By the favours of your Lord. You are not a mad man or insane as people claim. Surely you will get your reward that will never cease, your rewards are endless which have no limits.[1] Surely, you are of sublime character."[2]

ʿĀ'ishah ﷺ was once asked, "Can you describe some of the characteristics of the Messenger of Allāh ﷺ?" She replied, "His personality was the Qur'ān."[3] He was a living Qur'ān; whatever Allāh ﷻ has commanded, he obeyed. It is important to note that the Qur'ān isn't merely compromised of legislation pertaining to prayer, fasting, giving alms and performing pilgrimages. Rather, it bears guidance which can direct a person throughout their life. It advises us as to how we should lead our social life and how we should deal with the people around us. For example, Allāh ﷻ has listed many such ideals by which a person can save themselves from wrongdoing and lead a righteous life. He ﷻ has said:

"Your Lord has decreed that you worship none but Him, and do good to parents. If any one of them or both of them reach old age, do not say to them: uff [a word or expression of anger or contempt] and do not scold them, and address them with respectful words."[4]

"Do not kill your children for fear of poverty."[5]

"Do not go near fornication for it is an indecent deed and an evil way."[6]

"And do not take life - which Allāh has made sacred - except for a just cause."[7]

"And do not go near an orphans property except in the most fitting manner. (i.e. to improve it and increase it for him.)"[8]

---

[1] An insane person does not receive reward for their actions because of their illness. Likewise, Allāh ﷻ does not hold the insane person to account if they err. In this verse, Allāh ﷻ is indicating that if the Noble Prophet ﷺ was a mad man, how then would Allāh ﷻ reward him? The reason he is being rewarded is because of his magnificent sublime character, good deeds and worship.

[2] Al-Qur'ān 68:1-4

[3] Ṣaḥīḥ Muslim

[4] Al-Qur'ān17:23

[5] Al-Qur'ān 17:31

[6] Al-Qur'ān 17:32

[7] Al-Qur'ān 17:33

[8] Al-Qur'ān 17:34

"Give full measure when you measure, and weigh with a balance because that is the straight that is better and fairer in final determination. Do not pursue that of which you have no knowledge, surely, the hearing, the straight, the heart- all of those shall be questioned of"[1]

"People should not make fun of other people. Maybe those whom you are making fun of are better than you. Women should not make fun of other women. Maybe the other women are better than those who are making fun. Do not give bad names (nicknames) which would hurt the other person and stay away from thinking bad of other people. Do not investigate and butt in to other people's affairs! Do not backbite one another. Would you like to eat the flesh of your dead brother? You would abhor it."[2]

Thus, Shaykh ʿIzz ad-Dīn ibn ʿAbd al-Salām highlights that the Noble Prophet ﷺ had tremendous character and mannerisms. Allāh rewards people according to their characteristics. Religion and Islam consists of more than ritual worship, it is a complete way of life. In one ḥadīth it is mentioned, "The weightiest deed to be placed on the scale will be good manners."[3] Likewise, another ḥadīth says, "Surely, a servant [of Allāh] achieves the rank of one who fasts and prays through the night by [showing] good manners." An example of such a person would be the first caliph, Abū Bakr. His mannerisms were such that Saʿīd ibn al-Musayyib once exclaimed, "Abū Bakr did not gain more virtue over you [all] by excessive praying and fasting. He gained superiority over you because of something that was in his heart!"

What was in his heart? The Messenger of Allāh ﷺ was once in a gathering when he asked the Companions in attendance, "Who from among you has visited a sick person today?" They all remained silent apart from Abū Bakr who raised his hand and replied affirmatively. Thereafter the Noble Prophet ﷺ enquired, "Who from among you has fed a poor person today?" Once again, they all remained quiet apart from Abū Bakr who raised his hand. Then, the Messenger of Allāh ﷺ asked, "Who from among you followed a funeral procession today?" They all remained silent apart from Abū Bakr who once again raised his finger

[1] Al-Qur'ān 17: 35-36

[2] Al-Qur'ān 49:11-12

[3] Sunan at-Tirmidhī

and said, "There was a poor person who had died... I heard and I partook in his funeral procession." Upon hearing this, the Messenger of Allāh ﷺ said, "When these qualities, collectively prevail in a person, he will surely enter *Jannah.*"[1] This statement of the Messenger of Allāh ﷺ is symptomatic to the fact that Abū Bakr ؓ will enter *Jannah* due to the great characteristics he has possessed. Each of the questions that the Messenger of Allāh ﷺ asked were in regards to communal rapport as opposed to ritual worship. Therefore, it would be foolish to ignore the importance of bearing such great qualities.

These are some of the characteristics that make a good person and this is why Shaykh ʿIzz ad-Dīn ibn ʿAbd al-Salām ؒ has made mention of the Noble Prophet's ﷺ mannerisms. As he had the best character, he gained the highest rank in the eyes of Allāh ﷻ. Subsequently, he will be rewarded the most by Allāh ﷻ.

The Banner of Praise Will Be in His ﷺ Hand

2. **One of the favours granted to him is found in the words of the Messenger of Allāh ﷺ, "The Banner of Praise will be in my hand on the Day of Rising, and it is no boast."**

The ḥadīth mentioned in this passage can be found in *Ṣaḥīḥ Muslim.* When Allāh ﷻ comes for the Reckoning, the Banner of Praise will be given to the Messenger of Allāh ﷺ. All of humanity will stand behind this flag.

All Prophets Will Gather Beneath His ﷺ Banner

3. **One of the favours is found in the words of the Prophet ﷺ, "All Prophets, Ādam and those after him, will be under my banner on the Day of Rising, and it is no boast." These special qualities indicate his high rank above Ādam and others, since the only meaning of being shown preference is by being singled out for virtues and ranks.**

In fact, he said in one ḥadīth, "I will be the first to intercede."[2] Initially, nobody

[1] Ṣaḥīḥ Muslim

[2] Sunan at-Tirmidhī

will have the courage to speak to Allāh ﷻ. He will speak to Him on behalf of the whole creation.

The Messenger of Allāh ﷺ is Sinless

4. **One of them is that Allāh, exalted is He, told him that he has forgiven his past sins and future wrong actions. It is not transmitted that Allāh told any of the Prophets anything like that. It is clear that He did not tell them that because in the Standing when each of them is asked to intercede, he will mention the error which he committed and will say, "Myself! Myself!" If any of them had known that his error would be forgiven, they would not have been alarmed at it in that position. When people ask the Prophet ﷺ to intercede in that Station, he will answer, "I will do it."**

The term **'anything like that'** is in reference to the first verse of Sūrah Fatḥ wherein Allāh ﷻ has said:

> *"Surely, we have given to you a manifest victory, so that Allāh may forgive you for any mistakes you have made in the past or you will make in the future and so that Allāh may complete His favours and blessings upon you so that He may guide you upon the straight path and that He may assist you with a powerful assistance."*[1]

Allāh ﷻ has mentioned the word *dhanb* in this verse which some translate as 'sins'. I have used the term 'mistakes' otherwise the translation would become, "Allāh ﷻ has forgiven your sins." This then gives rise to the foolish who claim that the Messenger of Allāh ﷺ would sin. This is quite simply a mistake and a misunderstanding of Arabic language. The words that are used to describe sinning or making mistakes vary in the Arabic language. For example, there are four words which denote a mistake. They are *dhanb, sayyi'ah, mʿaṣiyah* and *khaṭa* ʾ.

Each of these words have connotations of 'making a mistake' but they rank differently in severity. The terms *mʿaṣiyah* and *khaṭa*ʾ are of the highest rank and denote sin. The term *dhanb* denotes something minor, a small mistake. For example, if a prophet has an option to commit to two deeds, he should select that which is

[1] Al-Qur'ān 48:1-3

superior. If he does something of less virtue, then Allāh ﷻ will regard it as a mistake. This is the context of the verse at hand.

For example, after the Battle of Badr, captives of war were brought to Madīnah Munawwarah where a consultation was held in order to determined what the Muslims should do with them. They had never been in such a position before! Abū Bakr as-Ṣiddīq ؓ and the majority of the Companions ؓ were of the opinion that they should be dealt with gently and that ransom should be exacted. Eventually all of the captives were freed. Some paid ransom, whilst others were instructed to teach children to read and write. Ten children were given to one captive and when they had becoming proficient in literacy, the captives were freed.

As mentioned previously, most of the Companions ؓ were inclined towards a lenient approach. However, ʿUmar ibn al-Khaṭṭāb ؓ said, "No, O Messenger of Allāh! These are the very people who persecuted us for thirteen years in Makkah al-Mukarramah and snatched out properties from us! They took our lands, our houses, our wealth and they drove us out of Makkah al-Mukarramah in the very clothes which we were wearing! Without any possessions! We should deal with them strictly and kill all of them!"

ʿUmar ibn al-Khaṭṭab ؓ then said, "You should give my relative to me and I will chop his head off! You should give ʿAqīl to ʿAlī (who is his brother) and he will deal with 'Aqīl. I think you should give so and so to so and so; they will deal with them." The Messenger of Allāh ﷺ was somewhat taken aback. He reaffirmed the position of leniency and did not pursue ʿUmar's ؓ opinion. After a few days, Allāh ﷻ revealed the verse:

> *"It is not fitting for a prophet that he should have prisoners of war until he has thoroughly subdued the land. You look for the temporal goods of this world; but Allāh looks to the Hereafter. And Allāh is exalted in might, wise. Had it not been for a previous ordainment from Allāh, a severe punishment would have reached you for the (ransom) you took."*[1]

The Noble Prophet ﷺ was shaken by this verse and exclaimed, "If the punishment [of Allāh ﷻ] had transpired, none besides ʿUmar would have survived." This was due to the fact that his (ʿUmar ؓ) verdict coincided with the opinion of Allāh ﷻ. This is

---

[1] Al-Qur'ān 8:67

an example of when the Noble Prophet ﷺ might have chosen something of less virtue. Nevertheless, Allāh ﷻ has said that he has forgiven him in the verse mentioned previously.

ʿUmar ؓ Sits by the Grave of the Messenger of Allāh ﷺ

After the death of the Messenger of Allāh ﷺ, ʿUmar ibn al-Khaṭṭāb ؓ was once sitting by the grave of the Noble Prophet ﷺ in Madīnah al-Munawwarah. As he was reminiscing, he said "O Messenger of Allāh ﷺ! How lofty is your rank in the eyes of Allāh ﷻ as when He mentioned one minor error of yours, he first pardoned you and then mentioned the mistake. He said in Sūrah at-Taubah:

> *"(O Prophet), Allāh has forgiven you; why did you permit them (to stay in Madinah) before the truthful ones could become distinct to you, and you could be sure of the liars?"*[1]

"O Messenger of Allāh! How high is your rank in the eyes of Allāh ﷻ as when He mentioned the prophets, He mentioned you first and thereafter mentioned the rest. He said:

> *"And remember when we took from the prophets their covenant; and from thee, from Nūḥ, Ibrāhīm, Mūsā, ʿĪsā, the son of Maryam. And we took from them a solemn covenant."*[2]

"O Messenger of Allāh! How can I describe you and your rank in the eyes of Allāh ﷻ? When the pulpit was constructed and you came out on Friday to give the *khuṭbah*, you ascended upon it and passed by the trunk of the palm tree on which you previously leaned on as you delivered your sermon. When this happened it began to cry and the entire mosque heard the wailing of that wood! It began crying upon your separation. You had to come down and console it by saying that you would supplicate to Allāh ﷻ that He will include it from among the trees of *Jannah*. O Messenger of Allāh ﷺ... today your *Ummah* is crying and today they are in need of your blessings, supplication and consoling."

The scholars of ḥadīth mention that the tree trunk remained there for many years

[1] Al-Qur'ān 9:43

[2] Al-Qur'ān 33:7

after that incident and was also there during the time of Abū Bakr and ʿUmar. After that, it was kept by Ubayy ibn Kʿab and then continued to remain in Masjid an-Nabawī. As far as I can remember, after a few centuries, there was once a fire in Masjid an-Nabawī. Many things were burnt and in that fire, the tree trunk was also burnt. This story has been narrated by Shaykh al-Hadīth Muḥammad Zakariyyā towards the end of his book *'Faḍail e Durūd Sharīf'*.

The State of the Prophets on the Day of Qiyāmah

Shaykh ʿIzz ad-Dīn ibn ʿAbd al-Salām then mentions the state of the prophets on the Day of Standing. People will request the prophets to ask Allāh to initiate the reckoning. They will first go to Ādam saying, "You are the first human being, ask that Allāh commences the Reckoning." He will say, "Myself! Myself!" He will mention the mistake he had made and highlight Allāh's anger. Thus, he will send them to Nūḥ.

Nūḥ will say, "I asked Allāh regarding something I should not have asked when I said, 'O Allāh! You promised that you will save my people, my family. My son is from my family and your promise is true and you are the Most Just among those who judge.'[1] Allāh replied, 'He is not from your family.[2] His actions are not correct.' Do not ask from me that for which you have no knowledge, I counsel you lest you become one of the ignorant."[3] Nūḥ will then advise the people to ask Ibrāhīm."

Ibrāhīm will mention that he had lied three times and therefore is not suitable to fulfil this duty. The first was when he said that he was ill to his community when they had invited him to participate in their festival. The scholars of ḥadīth say he might have meant this in the meaning of, 'my heart is sick due to observing your *shirk* (joining partners unto Allāh).'

The second lie was when he broke all the idols apart from the main one and placed an axe around its neck. When he was asked as to who did this, he replied, "The big one did it (i.e. people's worship of him caused his destruction)!"

The third lie occurred when he migrated from his birthplace of Babylon to Egypt

---

[1] Al-Qur'ān 11:45

[2] A prophet's family consist of those who follow him and are upon the right path.

[3] Sūrah Hūd 11:45-46

with his wife Sārah. When they arrived in Egypt, someone informed the evil King that a man has entered the city and with him is an extremely beautiful woman. The king had evil intentions so he summoned Ibrāhīm to him. He asked him who this woman was but he sensed that something was wrong and so he replied, "She is my sister." If he had said that Sārah was his wife, they would have killed him. He returned to Sārah and explained what had happened and told her that she is his sister in faith as they were the only two believers in that area, at that time. Thus, when she was called over to the King, Ibrāhīm performed ablution and began praying to Allāh. Sarah also began praying in the room in which she was held.

When the ruler entered, he found Sārah praying to Allāh and when he approached her, he was overcome by a seizure. Whilst in this state he said, "What have you done to me?! Let me go! I will not do anything to you!" Sārah saw this and said, "O Allāh, let him go, if anything happens to him then the people will say that I killed him." Subsequently, Allāh took the seizure away from him and he returned to his original state. He then attempted to approach her for a second time and the same thing happened. At this point, he may have been sincere in his saying that he will not harm her as he went out of the room and complained, "What have you people brought to me? She is not a human being! She is like a demon! She has cast a spell on me! Get rid of her and to take this spell away, give her some gift!"

Sārah then returned to Ibrāhīm with Ājar who was presented as a gift. When she arrived, Ibrāhīm who was still engaged in his prayer, could not control himself. During his prayer he looked at Sārah and gestured to ask her as to what had transpired. She said, "All praise is to Allāh! He protected me and dealt with that disbeliever!"

This is the reason as to why Ibrāhīm will be afraid on the Day of Standing. He will advise people to go to Mūsā.

Mūsā will also recall his mistake and will say, "I hit a man and he died! Go to ʿĪsā." ʿĪsā will say, "My people took me as God and as the son of God. Go to Muḥammad! He is such a person that Allāh pardoned him for any mistakes that he made in the past and any which he may have done in the future, he is a person who is forgiven, so go to him."

Thus, people will come to the Messenger of Allāh and he will say, "I am for this [task], I am for this [task]!" He will then proceed to the court of Allāh, fall prostrate before him and praise Him in such a manner that no one has ever praised Him before. Thereafter, Allāh ﷻ will start the Reckoning.

This is the crux of our discussion; had Allāh ﷻ said to the other prophets that they were pardoned for any previous or future mistakes, they would have proceeded to ask for the initiation of the Reckoning. However, they will all refuse and refer the matter to the Messenger of Allāh ﷺ. Once again, this shows his virtue over the other prophets.

The scholars have deliberated over the reason as to why the people will not come to the Messenger of Allāh ﷺ first. Perhaps the wisdom in coming to him last is so that other nations will not be able to say, "What has he done? Our prophets could have done this as well!" As they will have gone to every other prophet first, they will not be able to make this statement.

The Messenger of Allāh ﷺ will be the First to Intercede

5. Another favour is that the Prophet ﷺ is the first to intercede and the first whose intercession will be accepted. This indicates that he is singled out and preferred.

After the Messenger of Allāh ﷺ, other prophets will also offer their intercession but his will be the first to be accepted.

~ End of Session Two ~

Session Three

The Twelfth of Rabʿī al-Awwal

Today is the twelfth of *Rabʿī al-Awwal*, the day in which the Messenger of Allāh ﷺ was born, the day in which he migrated from Makkah al-Mukarramah to Madīnah al-Munawwarah and the day in which he passed away. The majority of the scholars say that he was born on the twelfth of *Rabʿī al-Awwal* which was a Monday. He also migrated to and reached Madīnah al-Munawwarah on a Monday and he passed away on a Monday which was also the twelfth of *Rabʿī al-Awwal*.

He ﷺ Reserved His Supplication for the Intercession

6. Among the favours is that the Prophet ﷺ preferred others to himself since every prophet was given a supplication which was answered and each of the prophets hastened his supplication in this world but the Prophet ﷺ kept his supplication as intercession for his community.

This is in reference to a ḥadīth in which the Messenger of Allāh ﷺ said, "Every prophet was given one supplication which would be readily answered. Every prophet hastened with his supplication [for a variety of reasons]. I have reserved my supplication for the intercession [i.e. of my *Ummah]*."[1]

It is mentioned in the Qur'ān that Nūḥ ﷺ invited his people to accept Allāh ﷻ as their lord for a prolonged period; he called them towards his way for nine hundred and fifty years! Allāh ﷻ told him that none would place belief in him apart from those who have already believed. Upon receiving this information, he supplicated to Allāh ﷻ which resulted in the destruction of those who had rejected his call. The conversation between Allāh ﷻ and Nūḥ ﷺ has been documented in the Qur'ān in the following manner:

"And it was revealed to Nūḥ: None of your people would come to believe any more, except

[1] Ṣaḥīḥ Muslim

those who have already believed. So, be not distressed by what they have been doing. And make an ark under Our eyes and according to Our revelation; and do not speak to Me about those who have crossed the limits, as they are destined to be drowned."[1]

And said Nūḥ, 'My Lord, do not leave on earth even a single inhabitant (surviving) out of the disbelievers. If You leave them (surviving), they will lead Your servants astray, and will beget none but a sinful disbeliever.' "[2]

His supplication was accepted and they were wiped out from the face of the earth. Similarly, Ibrāhīm ﷺ utilised his supplication when he said:

"My Lord, make me steadfast in Prayer, and my offspring as well. And, Our Lord, grant my prayer. Our Lord, forgive me and my parents and all believers on the day when reckoning shall take place."[3]

Other prophets also used their supplications during their lifetime but the Messenger of Allāh ﷺ has reserved this for the Day of Standing. He will request Allāh ﷻ to commence the Reckoning and to forgive his *Ummah.*

Allāh ﷻ Took an Oath on the Messenger of Allāh's ﷺ Life

7. One of them is that Allāh, exalted is He, swore by his life ﷺ and said, "*By your life, they were wandering blindly in their drunkenness.*" (15:72) Oaths made by the life of the one sworn by, indicate the honour and preciousness of his life in the sight of the One Who swears by him, and that his life ﷺ is worthy of being the object of an oath because of the general and particular blessing it contains, and this is not established about anyone besides the Prophet ﷺ.

This is in reference to the verse of Sūrah al-Ḥijr wherein Allāh ﷻ mentions the story of Lūṭ ﷺ and the deviance of his people.

---

[1] Al-Qur'ān 11:36-37

[2] Al-Qur'ān 71:27-28

[3] Al-Qur'ān 14:40-41

Allāh ﷻ Called the Messenger of Allāh ﷺ by the Most Beloved of Names

8. **Another favour is that Allāh, exalted is He, showed respect for him when addressing him and called him by the most beloved of his names and most radiant of his qualities, saying, "*O Prophet*" (8:64, 65, 70 and other places), "*O Messenger*" (5:41, 67) This quality is not established about anyone else, but rather is established that each prophet was called by his name. He exalted is He, says, "*And We said, Ādam, live, you and your wife in the Garden.*" (2:35) "*ʿĪsā son of Maryām, remember My blessing to you*" (5:110) "*Mūsā, I am Allāh*" (28:30) "*O Nūḥ , descend with peace from Us.*" (11:48) "*Dāwūd, We have made you a caliph in the land*" (38:26) "*Ibrāhīm, you have fulfilled the vision*" (37:105) "*Lūṭ, we are messengers from your Lord*" (11:81) "*Zakariyyā, We give you the good news*" (19:7) and "*Yāḥyā, take the Book strongly*" (19:12).**

It is obvious to everyone that when a master addresses one of his slaves by his most sublime attributes and radiant characteristics, while addressing others by their proper names that do not signify a quality or a characteristic, the position of the one addressed with the most sublime names and qualities is dearer and closer to him than the one he calls by his proper name. This is known from custom. If someone is called using the best of his qualities and characteristics, all of that emphasises his esteem and respect for him, so much so that one person said: Do not call me other than 'O her slave!' for it is the best of my names.

Allāh ﷻ has addressed the Messenger of Allāh ﷺ in various places in the Qur'ān. For example, He said:

> *"O Prophet, We have sent you as a witness and as a bearer of good news and a warner, and as the one who calls (people) towards Allah with His permission, and as a luminous lamp."*[1]

In this verse, Allāh ﷻ has addressed the Noble Prophet ﷺ by many of his qualities. He addressed him by saying, "O Prophet!" and then described him as a 'bearer of good news giver and as a warner'. The Messenger of Allāh ﷺ gave good

[1] Al-Qur'ān 33:45-46

news to those who are obedient to the commands of Allāh ﷻ and came to warn those who transgress His orders. Allāh ﷻ refers to the Messenger of Allāh ﷺ as '*the one who calls (people) towards Allah with His permission*' as he would invite people towards Allāh ﷻ by tongue. The Messenger of Allāh ﷺ would say, "O people! Say 'there is no god but Allāh' and you will be successful." He would go to people's residence and call them towards Allāh ﷻ.

The Radiance of the Messenger of Allāh ﷺ

The term '*luminous lamp*' which is mentioned in the verse is also a term used by Allāh ﷻ for the sun. The term lamp (*sirāj*) is used by Allāh ﷻ for the sun in other places within the Qur'ān. Allāh ﷻ says, "Did you not see how Allāh has created seven heavens one upon another and has made the moon a light therein, and made the sun a lamp?"[1]

Just as the sun brings light to the world, the Messenger of Allāh ﷺ was a lamp that illuminated the hearts of humanity. Wherever he went, he brightened that area. Even now, wherever his message goes, people's hearts are filled with light. Subsequently an Urdu poet has said:

قدم قدم پہ برکتیں نفس نفس پہ رحمتیں
جہاں جہاں سے وہ شفیع عاصیاں گزر گیا
جہاں جہاں گزر ہوا وہاں وہاں سحر ہوئ
جہاں گزر نہ ہوا وہاں ہے رات آج تک

درّ فشاني نے تیرے قطروں کو دریا کردیا
دل کو روشن کردیا انکھوں کو بینا کردیا
خود نہ تھے جو راہ پر اوروں کے رہبر بن گئے
وہ کیا نظر تھي جس نے مردوں کو مسیحا کردیا

[1] Al-Qur'ān 71:15-16

Wherever he set his foot, Allāh ﷻ sent blessings, and wherever his blessed presence went, Allāh ﷻ sent mercy.
[This happened] Wherever the one who intercedes for the sinful passed by.
Wherever he passed, dawn struck.
And wherever he did not go, there is darkness there till today!

It is your spreading of the pearls and jewels throughout the world that made drops into oceans,
it enlightened hearts and gave sight to the eyes.
Those who were not on the right path themselves became torchbearers of guidance for others.
What a gaze must it have been for the [spiritually] dead to then be able to revive others [spiritually].

Another poet says,

نبي کے خلق عظیم تر نے سبھي کو اپنا بنا کے چھوڑا
وہ لوگ جن میں درندگی تھی انھی کو رہبر بناکے چھوڑا
عمر تھے غصّے میں چوڑ اتنا چلے تھے حضرت کو قتل کرنے
مگر رسالت کی ایک نظر نے انھی بھی اپنا بنا کے چھوڑا

"His characteristics were such that he made everyone his own,
those who possessed animalistic traits, he turned them into torchbearers of guidance.
'Umar was furious to the extent that he proceeded to kill the Noble Prophet ﷺ!
But one glance at the Message made him one of them [and a guide for others]."

Allāh ﷻ Granted the Messenger of Allāh ﷺ Protection

Moving back to the discussion in contention; Allāh ﷻ says in another verse:

"O Messenger, convey all that has been sent down to you from your Lord. If you do not, then you shall not have conveyed His message (at all). Allāh shall protect you from the people. Surely, Allāh does not lead the disbelieving people to the right path."[1]

Allāh ﷻ guaranteed him protection in this verse; the Messenger of Allāh ﷺ was persecuted in Makkah al-Mukkaramah and when he migrated to Madīnah al-Munawwarah, there were many disbelievers and hypocrites who remained ardent to kill him. Consequently, he had security around him as he slept during the night. Once, he was lying restlessly when he wished that someone was there who would keep watch so that he could sleep. Immediately, he heard the sound of weaponry and asked, "Who is it?" Sʿad ibn Abī Waqās ؓ appeared and said, "It is me, I was lying down and thought I should come, keep guard and watch over you." Thereafter, the Messenger of Allāh ﷺ thanked him and slept.

This incident occurred during the earlier days of Islam. Thereafter, Allāh ﷻ revealed the verse, *"Allah shall protect you from the people."*[2]After this, the Messenger of Allāh ﷺ slept without anybody keeping guard.

Shaykh ʿIzz ad-Dīn ؒ finishes the passage mentioned above by stating, "**...so much so that one person said: Do not call me other than 'O her slave!' for it is the best of my names."**

This is in reference to poetry of al-Mutanabī. The meaning of the couplet is clear; when one is addressed with a desired pseudonym, they are thrilled. In some instances, calling a person by their name may demonstrate a lack of respect. Thus, when Allāh ﷻ addressed the Noble Prophet ﷺ by his attribute, He is actually highlighting the esteem in which He holds him in.

A King's Love for the Messenger of Allāh ﷺ

There was once a king by the name of Nāṣir ad-Dīn Maḥmūd. He had an attendant named 'Muḥammad' and every time he addressed him, he would call out, "O Muḥammad!" in a very loving and affectionate manner. The meaning of 'Muḥammad' is 'the praised one'. Once he called him by his nickname, 'Tāj ad-Dīn'; the attendant came, did what was required of him and then left the palace! After

[1] Al-Qur'ān 5:67

[2] Al-Qur'ān 5:67

a few days, he returned when he was summoned by the King. The King was somewhat disturbed and so he asked, "O Muḥammad! Where were you these past days? I have been missing you." His attendant replied, "You normally call me in an affectionate way. The way you said, 'Tāj ad-Dīn, go do this!' I thought that you might be angry with me or that I might have done something wrong. Consequently, I was disturbed, I did not know what to do and that is why I didn't come." The king replied, "My friend! Your name is 'Muḥammad' and every time I called you by your name, I have performed ablution. I never take the name Muḥammad without being in a state of purity. However, the day when I had to call you, I had not performed ablution and subsequently, I did not want to say Muḥammad without being in a state of purity. That is why I called you by your nickname, 'Tāj ad-Dīn'."Allāh is the Greatest! Such respect just for the name of the Messenger of Allāh ﷺ!

Similarly, the king Bahadur Shah Zafar passed away and after his death, somebody saw him in a dream and asked, "O King! How did you fare in front of Allāh ﷻ?" He replied, "Allāh ﷻ forgave me and was very kind to me." The person asked, "Is this because you were a very just king and ruler?" The King replied, "No, it was because of one deed that Allāh ﷻ liked immensely. I was on a journey when I came to a resting place. We stopped there and when I was about to sleep on my bed, I noticed that there was a Qur'ān on the shelf [ahead of me]. I could not spread my legs towards the Qur'ān and so I sat up immediately. I thought that I should perhaps move the Qur'ān from there and put it elsewhere but I thought better; I should not do that for the sake of my own rest. Thus, I tried to turn around and slept the other way but couldn't do so. Sometimes I was sitting down; at other times I was in another posture until I spent the whole night in a sleepless state because of the respect of the Qur'ān. I did not move the Qur'ān for my own sake and I couldn't sleep on the other side. Hence, Allāh ﷻ said to me, "O Zafar! I liked this deed of yours so much that because of it, I am forgiving you."

The Miracles of the Messenger of Allāh ﷺ Are Everlasting

9. Another favour he was granted is that the miracle of every prophet ceased and came to an end while the miracle of the Master of the first and last, namely the Immense Qur'ān, will remain until the Day of Rising.

He said in one ḥadīth, "There has not been a prophet among the prophets except that he was given signs by which human beings believe in. The miracle I was given was Revelation which Allāh revealed to me. [Subsequently,] I have great hope that on the Day of Standing, I will have the most followers."[1]

A prophet is like an ambassador; if a country's ambassador goes to another country, he has to present identification. In the same way, prophets are given tokens which take form as miracles. They are inimitable, and a sign of authenticity. The miracle of the Messenger of Allāh ﷺ is still with us today, people will continue to study it and will believe in him until the Day of Rising. This is what Shaykh ʿIzz ad-Dīn ﵀ ibn ʿAbd al-Salām ﵀ is affirming to in his statement.

Stones and Trees Would Converse With the Messenger of Allāh ﷺ

10. Another is the stones greeting him and the palm trunk sighing for him, and such events are not established about any of the other prophets.

The Messenger of Allāh ﷺ said, "Indeed, I still recognise the stone in Makkah which used to greet me before I was made a prophet."[2] The scholars differ when specifying the stone mentioned in the ḥadīth:

i. An-Nawawī ﵀ writes in his commentary of *Ṣaḥīḥ Muslim* that some commentators have said that this ḥadīth refers to the Black Stone (*al-Ḥajar al Aswad*) which is fixed on the corner of the Kʿabah. When a person starts their circamambulation of the Kʿabah, they must start from the Black Stone. It is a blessed stone that Allāh ﷻ sent down with Ādam ﵇ from Jannah. Orginially, it was whiter than milk but people kept on kissing it and rubbing their hands over it until, due to the sins of people, it turned black. That is why it is called the Black Stone. When the Messenger of Allāh ﷺ was a resident in Makkah al-Mukkaramah (before his Prophethood), he would pass by the Black Stone and many a times, he would hear it saying, "*Assalāmu ʿAlayka O Messenger of Allāh!*"

ii. The second opinion is that the stone is an ordinary stone that he saw on his way to the cave of Ḥirāʾ. The Messenger of Allāh ﷺ would go to this cave in order

---

[1] Ṣaḥīḥ al-Bukḥārī

[2] Saḥīḥ Muslim

to enjoy seclusion and privacy. Sometimes he would stay there for two to three weeks. The maximum amount of time he spent there was a month. As he would be returning, he would witness strange yet astonishing occurrences. At times, he would see light in front of him in the darkness of the night, and at other times, he would hear this stone saying to him, "*Assalāmu ʿAlayka O Messenger of Allāh!*" When he heard it for the first time, he began to look around but could not see anyone speaking to him, and so he was somewhat disturbed as to where this voice was coming from. Thereafter, he noticed that it was coming from the stone and after that, it became a routine that whenever he would use that path, the stone would greet him. This opinion has been narrated by as-Suyūṭī ؒ in his '*Khaṣā'is al Kubrā*'.

I mentioned the story of the tree trunk in the account of ʿUmar ibn al-Khaṭṭāb ؓ and therefore, it shall be omitted from our discussion at this juncture.

The Messenger of Allāh's ﷺ Were Unique

11. **Another one is that his miracles are distinguished from the miracles of others by a greater degree of inimitability, such as causing water to gush from between his fingers. This is a greater breaking of normal patterns than making water gush from a rock, because water does gush out of some rock structures. His miracle in making water gush from between his fingers is greater than its gushing from the stone of Mūsā ؑ.**

This is in reference to a ḥadīth which has been narrated in both *Ṣaḥīḥ al-Bukḥārī* and *Ṣaḥīḥ Muslim*. Anas ibn Mālik ؓ narrated that the Messenger of Allāh ﷺ was once in Madīnah al-Munawwarah, in a place called Zawrah when there was a need for water. He requested that a tub and some water be brought to him. He had the water poured over his hand and as soon as this happened, water started gushing out from between the blessed fingers of the Messenger of Allāh ﷺ until the whole tub was full. There was a group of approximately forty people present and they all performed their ablution from the water that gushed from the fingers of the Noble Prophet ﷺ.

At least five similar incidents are narrated in the books of ḥadīth. In fact, the likes of *al-Qāḍī* ʿIyyāḍ al-Mālikī ؒ have gone on to say that this event is a successive narration (*mutawātir*), an event which has been conveyed by numerous narrators thus making agreeability on its falsehood inconceivable. *Al-Ḥafiz* ibn Ḥajar has said it cannot be deemed successive but nevertheless, it has been narrated in many narrations [i.e. thus bearing credibility]. He has also scrutinised the authenticity of the narrations and has concluded that five of them are authentic.

Some Accounts of the Messenger of Allāh's ﷺ Miracles

Abū Qatādah says that when the Companions were on the expedition of Tābuk, which was one month's travel in going and returning, they passed by a place in the Arabian desert where they camped. There was no water and so the Messenger of Allāh ﷺ asked, "O Abū Qatādah! Where is that waterskin?" He replied, "O Messenger of Allāh ﷺ, it has dried out." The Noble Prophet ﷺ asked whether there was anything at all in the water skin, even if it be small. He replied, "O Messenger of Allāh! There is a little bit but if we try to pour it out, the skin might absorb it." The Messenger of Allāh ﷺ requested it and thereafter called for a tub to be brought. He rolled up his sleeve, placed his hand in it and said, "O Abū Qatādah! Pour the water [upon my hand]."

Abū Qatādah slowly poured a few drops onto the blessed hand of the Messenger of Allāh ﷺ and from in between his fingers, water started gushing forth like a fountain. Abū Qatādah says, "It [water] started coming out, gushing forth from between his fingers like fountains."[1]

Al-Ḥafiz ibn Ḥajar explains that this occurrence could have one of two explanations:

i. When he placed his hand in the tub; the water that was poured into the tub was increased due to the blessed hand of the Messenger of Allāh ﷺ.

ii. It actually came out from his fingers.

It is important to note at this point that this miracle was directly from Allāh. Just in the way it is He who can bring water out from dry land as fountains, He can bring out water from the body of the human being too. He has the power of, 'Be, and it comes to be'.

---

[1] Ṣaḥīḥ al-Bukḥārī

The Miracles of Mūsā 🕮

It is important to note that the second opinion is far greater in proving the miraculous nature of water coming out. Shaykh ʿIzz ad-Dīn 🕮 mentions this point as he compares the miracles of the Messenger of Allāh 🕮 with miracles of Mūsā 🕮.

When Mūsā 🕮 took Banū Isrāʾīl away from the persecution of Firʿaun and crossed the ocean, they came to a desert and were in dire need of food and water. Allāh 🕮 then sent down *mann* and *salwā* as sustenance for them. Allāh 🕮 said to Mūsā 🕮,

"When Mūsa sought water for his people, We said, 'Strike the rock with your staff!' And twelve springs gushed forth from it. Each group of people came to know their drinking place. Eat and drink of what Allah has provided, and do not go about the earth spreading disorder."[1]

Mūsā's 🕮 staff had a lot of power within it; he was once bathing in a pond or a river during the afternoon wherein people would be having their siesta nap (as is the norm in areas which have a hot climate). Hence, nobody was there so Mūsā 🕮 removed his attire, put it on a rock and he began to bathe himself. As he came out and motioned towards his clothes, the rock upon which his clothing rested began to run away. Mūsā 🕮 ran after it yelling, "O stone! Give me my clothes!" The stone scampered away until it came to a place where some of the leaders of the community were sitting and having a conversation. Previously, they had ridiculed Mūsā 🕮 for being modest and shy. They would say things like, "Why does he cover his body? Why doesn't he bathe as we do altogether? There must be something wrong with his body, he must have marks of lepropsy or perhaps his testicles are swollen." Allāh 🕮 wanted to establish that Mūsā 🕮 was complete and perfect in his stature. Thus, the stone led him there and they all saw his perfect body. Mūsā 🕮 took his clothes, covered his body, took his staff and started hitting the stone. He hit it seven to eight times! When narrating this incident, the Messenger of Allāh

---

[1] Al-Qurʾān 2:60

🌸 commented, "I swear by Allāh 🌸, the stone was bruised!"[1] This was another miracle connected to the staff of Mūsā 🌸.

It should also be borne in mind that prophets are created to perfection. One ḥadīth says, "Allāh has not sent a prophet except that he was handsome and possessed a beautiful voice. And your Prophet is the most handsome among them and the one with the most beautiful voice."[2] Illnesses may afflict a prophet in the form of a test like that which afflicted Ayyūb 🌸 but besides this, no prophet suffered from any defect.

The Messenger of Allāh 🌸 Restored a Companion's Eye

12. Another favour to him is that ʿĪsā 🌸 healed a blind person whose eye remained in its normal place while the Messenger of Allāh 🌸 restored an eye after it was hanging down on the person's cheek. This is a miracle in two ways:

One is that it was healed after it had been hanging down on his cheek. The second is that sight was restored to it after its loss.

This incident has been narrated by Abū Qatādah al-Ansārī 🌸 whose eye was hit by a weapon during the the the Battle of Uḥud. Consequently, his eye popped out of its socket and was hanging down upon his cheek. The people said, "Cut it off!" and Abū Qatādah al-Ansārī 🌸 said refused and came running to the Noble Prophet 🌸 and said, "O Messenger of Allāh 🌸! I've been injured!" The Messenger of Allāh 🌸 beckoned him closer, took his eye, prayed upon it and placed it in its socket. Abū Qatādah al-Ansārī 🌸 began to look around as if nothing had afflicted it. In fact, it became the stronger of his two eyes and when he grew old, the other eye weakened but this one remained strong. This account is true, it is narrated by a chain of narration which we can rely upon. I was reading a book, 'al-Āyyāt al-Bayyināt fī mā fī Aʿaḍāʾī Rasūl Allāh 🌸 min al Muʿjizah' – 'The Clear Signs about the Miracles in the Limbs of Messenger of Allāh 🌸' which discusses the blessed limbs of the Messenger of Allāh 🌸 and miracles that were attributed to them. For example,

---

[1] Ṣaḥīḥ al-Bukhārī
[2] Sunan at-Tirmidhī

Allāh ﷻ put blessings wherever his hand touched. He cured the eye of this companion ؓ by merely saying '...with the name of Allāh' and putting it back in.

Similarly, there was a companion by the name Salamah ibn al-Akwʿa ؓ who was also injured in a similiar battle. He was struck on his shin and people exclaimed, "Salamah is going to bleed to death!" He limped to the Messenger of Allāh ﷺ and showed him what had afflicted him. The Noble Prophet ﷺ passed his hands over his injury and Allāh ﷻ cured him, he felt no pain after that. He started walking as a normal person.

The Blessed Saliva of the Messenger of Allāh ﷺ

With regards to his ﷺ blessed saliva; whenever he applied it to something, it did the job of an anti-septic cream. As he was fleeing Makkah with his faithful companion Abū Bakr ؓ, they proceeded to a cave to lose the tail of those who were following them. Abū Bakr ؓ said, "O Messenger of Allāh ﷺ! Don't go into the cave! Let me go in first and check that everything is safe." He went inside, tidied it up but noticed there were holes in the ground. He took a piece of cloth and tore it into several pieces so that he could blocked the holes. Two holes were left and so he lay down and blocked them with his feet. It was only then when the cave was safe that he called called the Noble Prophet ﷺ inside. He said, "O Messenger of Allāh! Come, you may rest now." The Noble Prophet ﷺ rested his blessed head on the lap of Abū Bakr ؓ and fell asleep.

Now, as the Messenger of Allāh ﷺ slept, a snake appeared from one of the holes that Abū Bakr ؓ was blocking and bit him causing him immense pain. He refused to move because it would wake the Messenger of Allāh ﷺ and so he remained in his position but began to cry. The tears began to stream down his cheek and a few teardrops fell on the Noble Prophet ﷺ who woke up and enquired as to why Abū Bakr ؓ was crying. He said, "O Messenger of Allāh! Something has bitten me from inside this hole." Hence, the Messenger of Allāh ﷺ took his blessed saliva and applied it to the wound which immediately healed. After that, he travelled with the Noble Prophet ﷺ to Madīnah al-Munawwarah. This incident has been narrated by Shah Walī Allāh ad-Dehalwī ؒ and from him by al-Muftī Maḥmūd al-Ḥassan ؒ.

The Blessed Hair of Messenger of Allāh ﷺ

With regards to his ﷺ blessed hair; the likes of Khālid ibn al-Walīd ؓ mentions, "I had a few strands of his hair which I kept and had sewn into my hat. Whichever battle I would go to, I would wear that hat and Allāh ﷻ would grant us victory." It was due to the blessed hair of the Messenger of Allāh ﷺ.

Umm Salamah ؓ says that she too had a few strands of hair belonging to the Messenger of Allāh ﷺ. She put them into a silver container and whenever someone would be sick in Madīnah al-Munawwarah, they would send a bowl of water to Umme Salamah ؓ who would dip the container into the water. They would take the water, drink it and they would be cured.[1]

At times, Allāh ﷻ awards such miracles to those who follow His Noble Prophet ﷺ in totality. In one battle, Ḥājī Imdād Allāh al-Makkī and Maulānā Qāsim Nānotwī were fighting when the latter was struck by a bullet. Ḥājī Imdād Allāh al-Makkī placed his hand over that wound and he was cured immediately.

The Story of ʿIsā ؑ and a Young Man

As we are also on the topic of the miracles of ʿĪsā ؑ, I will narrate a story of young man who met him. He asked ʿĪsā ؑ whether he could spend time with him and the great prophet of Allāh ﷻ agreed. They had been travelling for a considerable amount of time when they came to a town. They were both hungry so ʿĪsā ؑ took some money out and instructed the man to purchase food from a nearby vendor. The man proceeded to purchase bread but realised that he was terribly hungry! As a result, he brought three pieces of bread but ate one surreptitiously. He then brought the remaining two with him. It is worthy to mention at this point that ʿĪsā ؑ was given the ability to see what people have consumed. Allāh ﷻ recalls this in the Qur'an wherein He says, *"I will tell you what you have eaten and what you have stored in your homes."*[2]

Thus, he was very aware of the situation at hand. As the man presented ʿĪsā ؑ with two pieces of bread, he asked him, "How many pieces of bread did you

[1] Ṣaḥīḥ al-Bukḥārī

[2] Al-Qur'ān 3:49

purchase?" He replied that he had purchased two pieces. ʿĪsā persisted, "Are you telling the truth?" He said, "Yes I am, I purchased only two." So they ate and then continued their journey.

On their way, they saw a leper and ʿĪsā prayed upon him, which resulted in him being cured. The young man said, "O ʿĪsā! This is a huge miracle!" ʿĪsā replied, "Yes but how many pieces of bread did you buy?" The young man replied, "I only brought two." How strange was the matter of this man? He was witnessing miracles but still lied to his prophet.

They continued their travel until they met a blind person. Once again, ʿĪsā blew on him and he was cured too. The young man once again exclaimed, "This is a magnificient miracle!" Again, ʿĪsā asked, "How many pieces of bread did you purchase? Tell me the truth." And once more, the young man lied.

Thus, they continued with their travel until they came to a place where they discovered three golden bricks. ʿĪsā asked the young man, "We have both found this gold so we have to share it. Correct?" The man replied, "Yes that is correct." ʿĪsā then said, "Now listen, if you tell me how many pieces of bread you bought, I will give you all of it." The young man immediately said, "I bought three and ate one on the way!" ʿĪsā stated, "You can take the golden bricks and do whatever you want with them but I am leaving you."

The young man was incredibly greedy and so he sat there and began to fantasise over his fortune. He began dreaming about the things he intended to purchase and began plotting a safe route home in order to evade thieves. As he began to plan his journey, three bandits emerged and noticed that he was in possession of a lot of gold! They immediately killed him and took the gold.

The three bandits sat down and felt extremely hungry and so they decided that two of them should keep guard of the gold whilst the other should get food. When one of them went to the town, Shaiṭān came to him and whispered to him that he should add poison to the food thus killing the other two. This would allow him to have all three bricks of gold for himself! He adhered to this and mixed poison into the food.

Meanwhile, the other two who were left behind planned that when their comrade returns, they should immediately kill him and keep the three pieces of gold for themselves! Thus, when he came with the food, they murdered him and then sat down to eat. They consumed the poison and so they died too!

Later that day, ʿĪsā ﷺ was returning from his journey and he passed by the area which now hosts four dead men scattered around three golden bricks. After observing this, ʿĪsā ﷺ said, "This is the reality of the world! This is the wealth people run after and nothing will come with us in the Hereafter apart from our deeds."

The Messenger of Allāh ﷺ Awoke the Spiritually Dead

13. One favour is that the spiritually dead who were brought from disbelief to the life of belief are greater than the number of those whom ʿĪsā ﷺ revived from physical death. What a great difference there is between the life of belief and physical life.

As I mentioned in the previous session, ʿĪsā ﷺ ressurected approximately seven people on several different occasions. Shaykh ʿIzz ad-Dīn ﷺ is saying that 'life' is of two types:

i. Physical Life
ii. Spiritual Life

The 'Spiritual Life' refers to bringing someone from disbelief to belief and such a life is far more valuable than the 'Physical Life'. Shaykh ʿIzz ad-Dīn ﷺ is articulating that the Noble Prophet's ﷺ bringing the spiritually dead back to life through belief is greater than feats of ʿĪsā ﷺ in physically bringing people back to life.

The Messenger of Allāh ﷺ Will Have the Largest Ummah and is Rewarded Through Their Good Deeds

14. Another favour is that Allāh, exalted is He, records a reward for every prophet according to the actions, states and words of his community, and his community will be half of the people of the garden, and Allāh, exalted is He, reported that his community is the *best community brought out to people.* Their being the best of all communities is because of the knowledge, goodly states, words and worship, statement or anything by which one draws close to Allāh, mighty is He and

exalted, that the Messenger of Allāh 🌸 directed people to and prayed for, he has the reward for it and the reward for whoever acts by it until the Day of Rising because of his 🌸 saying, "Whoever calls [others] to guidance has the reward for it and the reward for whoever acts by it until the Day of Rising." None of the [other] prophets reached this rank. It is reported in a ḥadīth, "Created beings are dependants of Allāh and the most beloved of them to Him are those who are the most beneficial to His dependants." Since the Prophet 🌸 was beneficial to half of the people of the Garden, and the other prophets were only beneficial to one section of the other half, his position 🌸 in nearness [to Allāh] is according to his position in being of benefit.

There is no gnostic of his community but that the like of reward of his gnosis is added to the gnosis of the Prophet 🌸.

There is no one in his community with a goodly state but that the Prophet 🌸 has the same reward for his state added to the states of the Prophet 🌸.

There is no one with a statement by which he draws near to Allāh, mighty is He and majestic, but that the Prophet 🌸 has the same reward for that statement added to his statements and his conveying of His Message.

There is no action by which one draws near to Allāh, mighty is He and majestic, whether of prayer, zakāh, setting slaves free, jihād, piety, dhikr, steadfastness, pardon and forgiving, but that the Prophet 🌸 has the same reward as the one who does it added to his reward for his actions.

There is no high degree or glorious rank which any of his community obtains by his guidance and direction but that the Prophet 🌸 has the same reward added to his degree and rank. That is multiplied because for those of his community who call people to guidance or initiate a good sunnah, he has the reward for that according to the number of those who act by it and then his multiplied reward goes to our Prophet 🌸 because he directed people to it and guided to it. This is why Mūsā 🌸 wept on the Night Journey with longing for the good fortune of the Prophet 🌸 since more of his community would enter the Garden than those of the community of Mūsā 🌸. He did not weep out of envious resentment as some ignorant people imagine, rather it was out of sorrow for what he had missed of a rank like his.

In this lengthy passage, Shaykh ʿIzz ad-Dīn 🌸 is saying that that the Messenger of Allāh 🌙 will be elevated because a prophet is ranked according to his followers. The Noble Prophet 🌙 said, "There will be a prophet from among the prophets [on the Day of Rising], only one individual from his community will have believed in him."[1]

He 🌙 said that, "On the Day of Standing, I will have the most followers." Likewise, he also said, "I saw a dream that there was a huge crowd which were covering part of the horizon. I thought that was my *Ummah*. I was told, 'No, that is the nation of Mūsā 🌙.' And then I was told, 'Look towards that side' and there was a great number of people. I was directed to another side and then another side and then I was told, 'This is your *Ummah*.'"

Shaykh ʿIzz ad-Dīn 🌙 also says, the Noble Prophet's 🌙 *Ummah* were made the **'best community brought out to people'**. Consequently, his own rank will be raised and he will have plenty of followers who will act upon his *Sunnah*, thus granting him the reward. He has said, "If someone introduces good *Sunnah* into Islam (a good way for people to follow), he will be rewarded for that and the reward of others who act upon it."[2] This ḥadīth indicates that not everything should classed as devious innovation.

Bidʿah and its Types

Shaykh ʿIzz ad-Dīn 🌙 was perhaps among the first to put innovations (*bidʿah*) into five categories:

i. *Wājibah*: It is obligatory (*wājib*) to initiate these innovations and to promulgate them. For example, the learning of various sacred sciences such as the principles of jurisprudence, ḥadīth studies, Arabic syntax and morphology etc. Similarly, the Companions 🌙 felt it necessary to write down the Qurʾān in the form of a book even though the Messenger of Allāh 🌙 did not do so.

ii. *Bidʿah al-Muḥarramah*: This is in reference to the innovations devised by devious sects. Since these sects invented beliefs which were contrary to the beliefs of the pious predecessors, they were classed as forbidden. Similarly, any addition to worship is an innovation. For example, praying four units for the Fajr prayer,

---

[1] Ṣaḥīḥ Muslim
[2] Ibid

or performing the Jummuʿah prayer on a Saturday. This will be classed as an innovation which is forbidden. It will be compulsory to refute the claims of such innovators.

iii. *Mustaḥab*: This is in reference to such innovations that did not necessarily prevail during the time of the Noble Prophet 🌸 however, the roots these acts are traceable and can be used to start something new. For example, constructing seminaries for education were not available during the time of the Noble Prophet 🌸, however there were circles of learning. This provides the framework for development. Such innovations are desirable.

iv. *Makrūḥ*: This is in reference to innovations which are disliked by the Sharia. For example, over embellishing mosques and spending fortunes on them when such an amount could be used for other noble causes. Similarly, beautifying the Qurʾān falls into this category according to the Shāfʿī school of thought. The Ḥanafī school of thought say that it is merely permissible.

v. *Mubāḥ*: This is in reference to innovations which are merely permitted by the Sharia. The Shāfʿī school of thought highlight it is merely permitted to shake hands with the person next to you after the Fajr and ʿAsr prayers in order to create harmony among fellow Muslims. However, the Ḥanafī school of thought class this as disliked. Similarly, extravagance in eating, drinking, living, wearing clothes etc falls into this category.[1]

The Night Journey and Ascension

Towards the end of the passage, Shaykh ʿIzz ad-Dīn 🪶 mentions the Night Journey. It comes in a ḥadīth which can be found in *Ṣaḥīḥ al-Bukhārī*, that when the Messenger of Allāh 🌸 was taken by Jibrīl 🪶 through the various stages of heaven, he met Mūsā 🪶 on the sixth heaven. He met other prophets aswell. On the first stage, he met Ādam 🪶, on the second he met ʿĪsa and Yaḥyā 🪶, on the third he met Yūsuf 🪶, on the fourth he met Idrīs🪶, on the fifth he met Ḥarūn🪶, on the sixth he met Mūsā 🪶 and on the seventh he met Ibrāhīm 🪶. Every prophet greeted him saying, "Welcome to the Pious Prophet, the Pious Brother."

The Prophet Mūsā 🪶 had a conversation with the Messenger of Allāh 🌸 before

---

[1] Mirqāt al-Mafātīḥ Sharḥ Mishkāt al-Maṣābīḥ

proceeding. When he moved on to the seventh heaven, Mūsā ﷺ began to cry and someone asked, "Why are you crying?" He replied, "This young man was sent as a prophet after me and more people will go to Jannah from his community than my community. That is what makes me cry."

Shaykh ʿIzz ad-Dīn ﷺ explains that this was not due to jealousy but it was because of the known fact that the more followers a prophet has, the higher his rank becomes. Consequently, the Noble Prophet's ﷺ followers will be more in number and Mūsā ﷺ will be the second after him.

The Messenger of Allāh ﷺ Was Sent to the Entire World

15. Another favour is that Allāh, mighty is He and majestic, sent every prophet to his own people while He sent our Prophet Muḥammad ﷺ to both jinn and mankind. Each of the prophet receives a reward for conveying his message to his community while our Prophet ﷺ will have the reward of conveying the message to everyone to whom he was sent, to some by directly conveying it and to others through those who conveyed it on his behalf, and that is why Allāh was gracious to him when He said, *"If We had wished We could have sent a warner to every town."* (25:51) The manner of the favour is that if Allāh had sent a warner in every town, then the Messenger of Allāh ﷺ would only have obtained the reward of his warning the people of his own town.

This theme can be found in various verses, Allāh ﷻ said:

"We have not sent you but as a mercy for the whole universe."[1]

"And We have not sent you (O Muḥammad) except as a bringer of good tidings and a warner unto all mankind; but most of mankind know not."[2]

"We have sent you to be a Messenger for the people. Allāh is enough to be a witness."[3]

On the contrary, other prophets were sent exclusively to their people. That is

---

[1] Al-Qur'ān 21:107

[2] Al-Qur'ān 34:28

[3] Al-Qur'ān 4:79

why when Mūsā ﷺ addressed Banū Isrā'īl, he would refer only to them. He said, *"O Children of Isrā'īl! I am a Messenger of Allāh unto you!"*[1] Likewise, other prophets would say, "O my people!" as has been documented in several places in the Qur'ān.

There is only one prophet who has asserted himself as a universal prophet. The Noble Prophet ﷺ said, "I have been given superiority [by Allāh] over the other prophets in six ways: I have been given brevity in speech, I have been assisted with awe, war booty has been made permissible for me, the earth has been made a place to offer prayer and gain purification for me and while a prophet was sent to his people specially, I was sent to the entirety of humanity. The succession of prophets ceased with me."[2]

Allāh ﷻ Spoke to the Messenger of Allāh ﷺ

16. Another is that Allāh, exalted is He, spoke to Mūsā ﷺ on Mount [Sinai] and in the Holy Valley and he spoke to our Prophet ﷺ at the Lote Tree of the Furthest Limit.

This occurred during the Night Journey when the Messenger of Allāh ﷺ reached a place known as the Furthest Limit which is located high above the seventh heaven. They came to a point where Jibrīl ﷺ informed the Messenger of Allāh ﷺ that he could not proceed any further. Thereafter, a beautiful couch-like seat was brought for the Messenger of Allāh ﷺ which had a green covering over it and he was made to sit on it before being taken to Allāh ﷻ. The Messenger of Allāh ﷺ said, "I ascended to an area where I could hear the inscribing of the pens."

This is the place where the Sacred Tablet, from which things are being noted down, is kept. The notes are then passed down to the angels of the lower heavens who take it and action the instructions that are given from it. They implement its command throughout the whole world.

Did the Messenger of Allāh ﷺ See Allāh ﷻ?

Beyond the Lote Tree is where Allāh ﷻ spoke to the Noble Prophet ﷺ and in some

---

[1] Al-Qur'ān 61:6

[2] Sunan At-Tirmidhī

narrations, he also witnessed His countenance. There is a difference of opinion with regards to that which I will mention briefly. There are four opinions:

i. The Noble Prophet ﷺ only spoke to Allāh ﷻ but did not see him.

ii. The Noble Prophet ﷺ observed Allāh ﷻ with his actual eyes.

iii. The Noble Prophet ﷺ observed Allāh ﷻ with the eyes of his heart. Al-Hāfiẓ ibn Hajar al-ʿAsqalānī said, "It was some type of witnessing that was gifted to him."

iv. This fourth opinion is of Abū al-ʿAbbās al-Qurṭubī, who writes that it is better to remain silent on this matter as it is not something regarding which we will be questioned in the Hereafter and so we should not deny it and nor should we try to prove it either.

However, Shaykh ʿIzz ad-Dīn could perhaps be of the opinion that he did not see Allāh ﷻ as he only mentioned 'talking' and 'conversing' with Him. He did not make mention of observing Him. Perhaps he would have mentioned that as well had that been his opinion.

The Ummah of the Messenger of Allāh ﷺ Will Be the First Enter into Jannah

17. Yet another favour is that the Prophet ﷺ said, "We are the last of the people of this world and we will be the first on the Day of Rising, who will be judged before other creatures and will be the first of those who enter the Garden."

I have explained this earlier in the morning session; on the Day of Rising, our Reckoning will be taken first and others will follow us.

The Messenger of Allāh ﷺ Will Be the First to be Resurrected

18. Another is that when He mentioned his leadership in general, He restricted it to the Day of Rising, so that he said, "I am the master of the descendants of Ādam on the Day of Rising, the first from whom the grave will be opened, and the first intercessor and the first whose intercession will be accepted."

When Isrāfīl will blow the trumpet for a second time, the first grave to open will be that of the Noble Prophet's ﷺ and he emerge from his grave. Alongside him will be Abū Bakr as-Ṣiddīq and ᶜUmar ﵄. They will proceed towards al-Baqīᶜ in Madīnah al-Munawwarah and its inhabitants will come out of their graves. They will then procceed to Makkah al-Mukarramah and to al-Maᶜālā where the inhabitants of those graves will rise. Together they will go to the Plane of Resurrection; people will start coming from other places and if they were buried in England, they will have to travel from here on foot! Some will arrive quickly, some will arrive late but everyone will get there in time for the Reckoning. They will be directed by Allāh ﷻ and there will be angels who will be guiding people, as Allāh ﷻ mentions: *"(They will see the reality) on the day in which the caller will call (them) to a gruesome object."*[1]

The Creation Will Humbly Petition for the Messenger of Allāh ﷺ

19. One favour of the Prophet ﷺ is that the whole creation will humbly petition for him on the Day of Rising, even Ibrāhīm ﵇.

This is in the ḥadīth of intercession which we mentioned.

Seventy Thousand of the Messenger of Allāh's ﷺ Community Will Enter into the Garden Without Reckoning

20. Another is that seventy thousand of his community will enter the Garden without reckoning, and that is not established about anyone else.

The Messenger of Allāh ﷺ once said, "Seventy thousand from among my community will enter into Jannah without reckoning, nor any punishment." The Companions ﵃ asked, "Who are they O Messenger of Allāh ﷺ?" He replied, "They are those who do not seek invocations to be read upon themselves. [They are] those who do not cauterize, and those who do not take bad omens. They rely upon their Lord."[2] One companion by the name of ᶜUkāshah ibn Miḥṣan ﵁ got up and said, "O Messenger of

---

[1] Al-Qur'ān 54:6

[2] Such individuals are pious godly human beings. If they were to fall ill, they would refuse the assistance of a doctor and put their complete trust in Allāh ﷻ. We should not be like this. Their obedience to Allāh ﷻ allowed them to progress to a high level of belief and as a result, Allāh ﷻ looked after them and cured them. We have been told to follow the *sunnah* of the Messenger of Allāh ﷺ which entails that we look after our health.

Allāh! Supplicate to Allāh ﷻ that he includes me amongst them." And the Messenger of Allāh ﷺ said, "O Allāh include him among them!"[1] Thereafter, another person stood up and said, 'O Messenger of Allāh! Supplicate to Allāh ﷻ that he includes me amongst them!" The Noble Prophet ﷺ replied, "ʿUkāshah has beaten you to the supplication."

A question arises as to why the Messenger of Allāh ﷺ did not supplicate for the other individual in this incident? The answer is that if he did, there would be an entire queue of people requesting the Noble Prophet ﷺ to supplicate for them! Hence, he explained that there was a time for supplications and it had been accepted for ʿUkāshah ﷺ.

Some narrations have stated that the Messenger of Allāh ﷺ further said, "With every thousand, seventy thousand [entered in to *Jannah*]." The number seventy thousand mentioned here is not an exact figure, the Noble Prophet ﷺ is merely expressing that exact number will be magnificent. We pray to Allāh ﷻ that He includes us among them and alongside His sincere believers. May He enter us into Jannah without any reckoning and punishment. *Āmīn.*

Ruqyah and Healing

Seeking invocations for protection (*ruqyah*) has also been mentioned in this ḥadīth. It should be understood that other ḥadīth permit seeking invocations and reciting them upon others. For example, if you pray verses from the Qur'ān, or phrases from the *aḥadīth* and then blow upon a sick person, Allāh ﷻ may cure them. Some may question as to how there can be benefit through merely praying and blowing?

ʿAlī ibn Sīnā Doubts Ruqyah

I recall an incident regarding Abū ʿAli ibn Sīnā (Avicenna); many of you must be aware of this name, especially students of medicine. His book, *'Al Qanūn fī aṭ-Ṭibb'* is very well known. He was an authority in his field and a great philosopher. He had

[1] ʿUkāshah ibn Miḥṣan ﷺ was a great companion of the Messenger of Allāh ﷺ. There is a famous miracle which has been attributed to him; during a battle, his sword was shattered and so the Noble Prophet ﷺ gave him a stick which turned into a sword. He then continued to use the sword throughout the day. He had it for as long as he lived and he used it throughout his lifetime. The sword was named, the Divine Aid (*al-ʿAwn*). He was from the tribe of Quraish from Makkah al-Mukarramah and died as a martyr.

studied Arabic language extensively alongside philosophy, logic and medicine but before he could move on to the study of sacred knowledge, he had become fixated in the aforementioned subjects. As a result, he began to author many publications about medicine but because of his study of philosophy, he said some controversial things that perhaps he should not have said in relation to faith. Eventually, he became distant from religion and discarded prayer.

Once it so happened that the Prince of his time was severely ill and the King did all he could do to cure him with various medicine but it was to no avail. Ibn Sīnā was the best in his field at that time and he failed to cure him. The Prince was virtually on his deathbed when a person came to the King and said, "There is a man by the name Shaykh Najm ad-Dīn al-Qīrī ﵀. He is a big scholar of our time... why don't you call him? Perhaps he can come and read something upon your son so that he may get better?" The King sent his representative with a message, "Shaykh, I would have loved to come to you but my son is very ill and I cannot leave him. Could you kindly come and perhaps read something on him?" The Shaykh arrived came and began observing the Prince who was lying on the bed. He then began to read the 'Verses of Healing' upon him[1] and blew upon the Prince. Ibn Sīnā was standing in one corner and sarcastically began to imitate Shaykh Najm ad-Dīn ﵀ whilst questioning, "What is going to happen with this blowing?! I have tried all these medicines and nothing has happened!" The Shaykh was infuriated, his face changed colour! He looked at Ibn Sīnā with such anger and said, "Unworthy! Dog! Scumbag! Filth! Who brought him over here?! This unworthy scum!" The face of Ibn Sīnā changed colour as he was humiliated and rendered speechless. The reality was that the great Shaykh had given him the answers to his question in those words of abuse. Shaykh Najm ad-Dīn ﵀ said, "I didn't hit you... so why has your face turned red? I have only said a few words of abuse. If

---

[1] The verses are as follows:

﴿ وَيَشْفِ صُدُورَ قَوْمٍ مُّؤْمِنِينَ ﴾ ﴿ يَا أَيُّهَا النَّاسُ قَدْ جَاءَتْكُم مَّوْعِظَةٌ مِّن رَّبِّكُمْ وَشِفَاءٌ لِّمَا فِي الصُّدُورِ وَهُدًى وَرَحْمَةٌ لِّلْمُؤْمِنِينَ ﴾ ﴿ يَخْرُجُ مِن بُطُونِهَا شَرَابٌ مُّخْتَلِفٌ أَلْوَانُهُ فِيهِ شِفَاءٌ لِلنَّاسِ ﴾ ﴿ وَنُنَزِّلُ مِنَ الْقُرْآنِ مَا هُوَ شِفَاءٌ وَرَحْمَةٌ لِّلْمُؤْمِنِينَ ﴾ ﴿ وَإِذَا مَرِضْتُ فَهُوَ يَشْفِينِ ﴾ ﴿ قُلْ هُوَ لِلَّذِينَ آمَنُوا هُدًى وَشِفَاءٌ ﴾

there can be such an effect in words of abuse, why can their not be any effect in the word of Allāh ﷻ?!"

The Method of Ruqyah Used by the Messenger of Allāh ﷺ

The Messenger of Allāh ﷺ would recite invocations and thereafter blow up himself. In fact, once he became ill and Jibrīl ؑ came to him and blew upon him. He came and said, "O Muḥammad! In the name of Allāh do I pray upon you. May Allāh cure you from every ailment that afflicts you, in the name of Allāh do I pray upon you."

Likewise, when Ḥassan and Ḥussain ؓ were ill, the Noble Prophet ﷺ would recite the following invocation upon them, "I seek protection for you in Allāh's perfect words from every devil, vermin, and every evil eye." He would blow this upon them and say that this is what Ibrāhīm ؑ would read upon Ismāʿīl and Isḥāq ؑ. Hence, such invocations are permissible but in the ḥadīth in contention, the Noble Prophet ﷺ is trying to emphasise the virtue of total reliance upon Allāh ﷻ. The ḥadīth informs us that we should not scamper here and there for amulets (*taʿwīdh*) but rather, one should maintain trust in Allāh ﷻ who is the Sustainer.

~ End of Session Three ~

Session Four

The Messenger of Allāh ﷺ Will Be Granted Wasīlah

21. Another favour granted to him is seen in his words: "The *wasīlah* is a station in the Garden which is only proper for one of the slaves of Allāh, exalted is He, and I hope that I will be him. If anyone asks for the *wasīlah* for me, intercession will be incumbent for him."

The Messenger of Allāh ﷺ said in relation to the supplication which is recited after the Call to Prayer, "When you hear the Caller (*mu'adhin*), repeat what he says, then invoke a blessing on me, for everyone who invokes a blessing on me will receive ten blessings from Allāh; then ask from Allāh *wasīlah* for me, which is a rank in Paradise fitting for only one of Allāh's servants, and I hope that I may be that one. Anyone who asks that I be given *wasīlah* will be assured of my intercession."[1] The supplication is as follows:

> *"O Allāh, Lord of this perfect call and established prayer. Grant Muḥammad the wasīlah and favour, and raise him to the honoured station that You have promised him, bless us with his intercession on the Day of Rising. Verily, You do not neglect promises."*[2]

This supplication is a combination of the various narrations mentioned in the ḥadīth. The words which are in discussion here are, "*Grant Muḥammad the wasīlah and favour.*"

Lexically, the word *wasīlah* denotes the meaning: a high rank with the king. For example, a minister has a lofty status in the eyes of the king and he is considered to be a trustworthy person. As a result of this trust, people will regard the position of

---

[1] Ṣaḥīḥ Muslim

[2] The Arabic is as follows:

اَللهُمَّ رَبَّ هَذِهِ الدَّعْوَةِ التَّامَّةِ والصَّلاَةُ القَائِمَةِ ، آتِ سَيِّدَنَا مُحَمّداً نِ الوَسِيْلَةَ وَالفَضِيْلَةَ وَابْعَثْهُ مَقَاماً مَحْمُوْدُ نِ الَّذِيْ وَعَدْتَّهُ وَارْزُقْنَا شَفَاعَتَهُ يَوْمَ الْقِيَامَةِ ، إِنَّكَ لاَ تُخْلِفُ الْمِيْعَادْ

the minister as a *wasīlah.* Therefore, if somebody wanted to approach a king for some reason, he would not go to him directly but rather, he would initiate dialogue with the minister. Thereafter, the minister would aid him by making mention of him to the king. The minister is typically aware of the manner in which he should approach the king and he would know how to persuade him too. The king would then act accordingly to what has been requested because the minister (who holds a position of proximity) is the one who has made the request.

Shaykh Aḥmad as-Sarḥindī ﵀ was a renowned reformer of his time. He revived the *Ummah* in the 'second millenium' after the Migration (*hijrah*). The spirituality of the *Ummah* was rocking and about to sink but it was Shaykh who seized the matter and rectified the state of many. The majority of Islam was being promulgated in the Indian subcontinent at the time. They were affluent and were responsible for looking after the two Sacred Mosques and the hajjis. This was the era when the Taj Mahal, Agra Palace were being constructed and a strong decline in practising Islam was felt. It was at this time that Shaykh Aḥmad ﵀ participated actively in bring people back towards the straight path to the extent that he was known as 'the Reviver of the Second Millenium'.

My Shaykh and teacher, Shaykh al-Hadīth Maulānā Yūsuf Motālā (may Allāh ﷻ protect him) once mentioned in his lesson that Shaykh Aḥmad ﵀ has written, "Once I prayed the Prayer of Need and supplicated to Allāh ﷻ to make *wasīlah* exclusive to the Messenger of Allāh ﷺ and to grant it to him. Allāh ﷻ accepted my prayers; I observed in a dream that Allāh ﷻ said, 'Your prayers have been accepted.'

My beloved Shaykh then commented, "This does not mean we should stop supplicating as we are bound by the Sharia. When the Messenger of Allāh ﷺ has said, 'Ask *wasīlah* for me.' We must continue asking till the Day of Rising."

The Messenger of Allāh ﷺ Will Be Granted the Fountain of al-Kawthar

22. Another favour is Kawthar which will be given in the Garden, and the Basin which he will be given at the Standing.

This passage is in reference to the fountain of al-Kawthar (the Pool of al Kawthar) which will be given at the Standing. The Messenger of Allāh ﷺ has said, "My fountain covers the distance between ʿAdn to Aylah, the distance of one month. Its water is whiter than milk, sweeter than honey and the utensils are more in number than the stars of the skies. Whosoever drinks from that pool will never feel thirsty ever again."[1]

The majority of the scholars of ḥadīth are of the opinion that The Messenger of Allāh ﷺ will receive this in the Plane of Gathering [i.e. the Standing] when He will proceed to Allāh ﷻ and request the Reckoning to start. It is at that time when he will be given al-Kawthar. People will drink from the fountain and then proceed for their Reckoning.

Throughout the Reckoning, individuals who have tasted water from the fountain will not feel thirsty but rather, they will be at ease. For some people, the Reckoning will be particularly short and there will be others who will be taken into Jannah without being put to trial at all. If one's life has been spent in a lavish and sinful manner, the Reckoning will be elongated. For every penny and every pound one earned, they will be asked as to where they spent it and accumulated it. Their every moment will be scrutinised.

Thereafter, the weighing of deeds on the scales will occur, the questioning and the Book of Deeds will be given in either the right hand or left hand. Those who receive their books in their right hand will enter Jannah and those who receive their books in their left hand will enter the Fire.

People will then have to cross the Bridge; after crossing it, people will gather at a place for the Messenger of Allāh ﷺ to arrive. He will come and take everybody with him into Jannah. He will be the first one to knock on the gates of Jannah. Riḍwān, the gatekeeper of Jannah, will ask, "Who is it?" He will reply, "I am Muḥammad, I have come with my *Ummah*." Riḍwān will confirm that he has been ordered to open the gate for the Noble Prophet ﷺ and his *Ummah* and thus it will be opened allowing us entry into *Jannah*.

The Messenger of Allāh's ﷺ Ummah Came Last But Are The Forerunners

23. Another one is expressed by the words of the Prophet ﷺ, "We are the last, the forerunners..." the last in time and forerunners in virtues and qualities.

[1] Ṣaḥīḥ al-Bukhārī

Spoils of War Was Made Lawful for The Messenger of Allāh's ﷺ Ummah

24. Another favour is that booty was made lawful for him while it was not made lawful for anyone before him...

Al-Imām Bukhārī narrates a ḥadīth in his *Ṣaḥih*; Yūshaᶜ ibn Nūn, who is the successor of Mūsā once engaged in a battle and after it was finished, there was war booty. The Divine order was such that whatever people had accumulated from the war booty should be gathered in one place. The prophet of that community would pray to Allāh and fire would descend from the sky subsequently burning the booty. This would be a sign that their effort was accepted by Allāh.

After the expedition, Yūshaᶜ ibn Nūn gathered the booty and prayed upon it but the fire did not descend. He realised that somebody had acted treacherously and had stolen from the war booty. He launched an investigation to find out who this person was. He said, "I want the leader of every tribe to come and pledge allegiance to me, put his hands in my hands." The leaders came and shook hands with him. As they were shaking his hands, one of their leader's hands had become stuck to the hands of Yūshaᶜ ibn Nūn. Yūshaᶜ said, "The treachery and theft has come from your tribe. I want people from your tribe to come and shake their hands with mine." They came one after the other and no sooner did the hands of the the thief stick to the hands of Yūshaᶜ. He said, "You have committed the theft!" His belongings were searched and they found a huge vase filled with golden coins that he had stolen from the war booty. They placed it in the open area with all the other booty. Then he (Yūshaᶜ ibn Nūn) supplicated upon it and the fire descended thus burning the booty. The reason why Allāh permitted its acquisition for us is because we needed it.

Tayammum

"...the rows of his community were made like the row of angels and the whole earth was made a mosque for him and its earth was made a means of purification. These special qualities indicate his high rank and the kindness [shown] to his community."

If a person is without water and the need to perform ablution whilst on a journey arises, or is in need of bathing to become pure again, they may perform *tayammum* and pray. *Tayammum* is performed by the striking of the hands on the earth, dusting them and then passing them over the face. Thereafter, it will be done a second time and the hands will be passed over the hands up to the elbows. This will be regarded as purification and it is a substitute for the ablution and bathing in the absence of water. It is important to note that *tayammum* is the same for both ablution and bathing. This was was not permitted for the people before us but has been allowed for this *Ummah*.

Allāh ﷻ Praised The Messenger of Allāh's ﷺ Character

25. One favour is that Allāh, exalted is He, praised his character and said, "*Indeed you are truly vast in character*" (68:4). When the great hold something in high esteem it indicates its immensity, so what of the case when it is esteemed by the Greatest of the great [i.e. Allāh ﷻ]?

This was discussed to a great degree in the first session. The character of the Messenger of Allāh ﷺ was impeccable and he was perfect in every way.

A person will be able to tell if another is insane by the way they converse and behave. Once, Ḥakīm Aflatūn was walking on the street and an insane person greeted him. Ḥakīm Aflatūn came home and took medicine for madness. He said, "Why did that mad man greet me?! There must be something wrong with me, I must be mad too and that is why he greeted to me!"

Allāh ﷻ Spoke to Him in Three Ways

26. Another is that Allāh, exalted is He, spoke to him with three types of revelation:

i. True Dream
ii. Direct speech without intermediary
iii. Through Jibrīl ﷺ

The True Dream – al-Imām at-Tirmidhī ﷺ narrates in his *Sunan* that the Messenger of Allāh ﷺ said, "I saw my Lord in the best of forms and He said, 'O Muḥammad! What is the matter regarding which the angels of the High Position are debating about?' I said, 'I don't know.'

Thereafter, its knowledge was made apparent to him and he gave the answer, "They are debating about the deeds which expiate a person's sins. They are: performing ablution in spite of disliking it,[1] going to the mosque frequently for prayers and waiting for prayers one after the other." This was an incident wherein he saw Allāh ﷻ in a dream. Allāh ﷻ knows best as to how the details of this dream and how it was made manifest to the Messenger of Allāh ﷺ.

Direct Speech – This was discussed earlier; the Messenger of Allāh ﷺ travelled on the Night Journey wherein he ascended, high above the heavens to Allāh ﷻ. It was here that he conversed with Him without an intermediary.

Through Jibrīl ﷺ - Jibrīl ﷺ would bring revelation to the Messenger of Allāh ﷺ and he came on many instances during a period of twenty three years. I cannot recall the exact number but some scholars have gone on to narrate the amount of times Jibrīl ﷺ came down with revelation. Some have said that he had come seven thousand times as he would come two to three times a day. He would visit the Noble Prophet ﷺ everyday during the month of Ramaḍān. He would revise the Qur'ān with the Messenger of Allāh ﷺ throughout this blessed month.

After the demise of the Messenger of Allāh ﷺ, Abū Bakr as-Ṣiddīq and ʿUmar ibn al-Khaṭṭāb ﷺ said to one another, "Let's go visit Umm Ayman like the Messenger of Allāh ﷺ would visit her." They both went to her house where she was weeping whilst reminiscing over the era of the Noble Prophet ﷺ. They said, "O Umm Ayman, why are you crying? You know the Messenger of Allāh ﷺ has gone to Allāh ﷻ and the reward which Allāh ﷻ has reserved for him is better than his staying in this world." So she replied, "I know that where he has gone is better than the place he was in but I am crying because Jibrīl ﷺ has stopped coming and because revelation has stopped coming. Due to revelation no longer being revealed, the mercy and the blessings that come with it have also ceased. This is what makes me cry." After they both heard this, they began to weep bitterly too!

However, Mūsā ﷺ conversed with Allāh ﷻ directly and perhaps through Jibrīl ﷺ too.

The Qur'ān is the Most Complete Scripture

---

[1] For example, due to the water being cold.

27. Another favour is that his Book contains what the Torah, Injīl and Zabūr contain, and he was granted the *Mufaṣṣal* as well.

In some cases, we see the exact words of the Qur'ān are that which are in the Torah as well, for example:

"...We decreed for the children of Isrā'īl that whoever kills a person not in retaliation for a person killed, nor (as a punishment) for spreading disorder on the earth, is as if he has killed the whole of humankind, and whoever saves the life of a person is as if he has saved the life of the whole of humankind.."[1]

"We prescribed for them therein: A life for a life, an eye for an eye, a nose for a nose, an ear for an ear and a tooth for a tooth; and for wounds, an equal retaliation. Then, if one forgives it, that will be expiation for him. Those who do not judge according to what Allāh has sent down, they are the unjust."[2]

In addition to that which is present in the other books, Allāh ﷻ gave the Messenger of Allāh ﷺ *Mufaṣṣal. Mufaṣṣal* is indicative towards the last chapters of the Qur'ān. The scholars of the Qur'ān have divided it into different sections in light of what has been mentioned within the ḥadīth. They are:

i. ***As-Sabuᶜ aṭ-Ṭiwāl*** – These are the seven long sūrahs include al-Baqarah, Āle ᶜImrān, an-Nisā, al-Mā'idah, al-Anᶜām, al-Aᶜrāf, al-Anfāl and at-Taubah (these two are considered as one).

ii. ***Al-Mi'īn*** - The sūrahs which have approximately one hundred verses or more.

iii. ***Al-Mathānī*** – The oft repeated sūrahs, for example like Sūrah al-Fātiḥah.

iv. ***Al-Mufaṣṣal*** – This starts from Sūrah Qāf, although others have said it starts from al-Ḥujurāt. The last four and a half chapters of the Qur'ān contain the sūrahs which are called al *Mufaṣṣal.*

The Gospel predominantly contains parables, examples, advice, counselling and good words. The Torah largely contains commandments as to what is

[1] Al-Qur'ān 5:32

[2] Al-Qur'ān 5:46

permissible and forbidden. There is a difference between them; however, the Qu'ran is a compilation of previous scriptures and more.

The Ummah Will Receive a Greater Reward Than Any Other

28. **Another is that his community has performed less actions than those before it but will receive a greater reward as is stated in sound ḥadīth.**

This ḥadīth is narrated by *al-Imām* Muḥammad 🏵 towards the end of his *'Muwaṭṭaʿ'* and it has also been narrated by *al-Imām* al-Bukhārī 🏵. That the example of the People of The Book before us is of a person who employed labourers for work from morning till noon. He then said, "I will give you one *qīraṭ* (pound) only." He thereafter employed others from noon to the forenoon and promised them one *qīraṭ* too. Then finally, he employed the last community of labourers from the forenoon to sunset said, "I will give you two *qīraṭ*." In the same way, Allāh 🏵 promised us that even though our deeds are less, we are promised more rewards. The previous nations before us did more deeds but their rewards were less. This is a special gift given to the *Ummah* of the Noble Prophet 🏵 by Allāh 🏵. They had considerable amount of time to do good but were rewarded less. Allāh 🏵 gave us the Night of Power and the likes of which they did not have.

So the first two nations objected! They said, "Our labour is more but our wages are less and their labour is less and their wages are more!" So Allāh 🏵 said, "Have I done injustice to you (by giving you less than what I promised)?!" They said, "No, You have given us what you promised." He 🏵 said, "Then if I give someone more, then that is My grace, I bestow it on whom I wish."

The Messenger of Allāh 🏵 Preferred Humility

29. **Among another of them is that Allāh, mighty and majestic is He, offered the keys to the earth's treasures and gave him the choice between being a prophet who was a king or a prophet who was a slave, and he consulted Jibrīl 🏵 who indicated, "Be Humble!" He said, "Indeed, [I will be] a prophet who is a slave. I will be hungry one day and full one day. When I am hungry, I will call on Allāh. When I am full, I will thank Allāh."**

The Prophet ﷺ intended to be occupied with Allāh both in times of hardship and ease, in blessing and affliction.

A servant is in the kitchen serving food, when he gets time, he quickly has a few morsels and then he moves on to serve the master if he is called upon. The Messenger of Allāh ﷺ was offered the treasures of the earth, he was told, "If you want them, then We can change the mountains of Makkah to gold and you can give that money to people and bring them to Islam." However, he knew that this would be a way of creating greed within people. Those who embraced Islam because of money will live thereafter on monetary progress. Once the money goes, their faith will too.

Islām is not centred upon the hoarding of wealth! You cannot spread Islām by wealth in hope that its recipient will change. Islam is a religion which is based on sacrifice and it captures the hearts of people. People embrace Islam and in effect they become closer to Allāh ﷻ and the Messenger of Allāh ﷺ. Islām was spread through sacrifice and not through wealth. Take a look at the early Muslims such as Bilāl, Khabbāb, ʿAmmār, Ibn Masʿūd and Salmān ؓ; they all were the strongest in faith but were tested severely. Their sacrifices are unparallel. Islām was not spread by the sword but was spread by its beliefs and principles. The ideology and the practicality of Islām captured the hearts of the people and this is what is being articulated by Shaykh ʿIzz ad-Dīn ؒ.

The Messenger of Allāh ﷺ Was Sent as a 'Mercy to All Beings'

30. **Another favour is that Allāh, exalted is He, sent him as a "*mercy to all beings*" (21:106) and so He gave respite to the rebels of his community and did not hasten their punishment, so that they were preserved, contrary to prophets before him. When they were denied, the punishment hastened for those who denied them. In respect of the qualities of the Prophet ﷺ: his forbearance, forgiveness, granting pardon, his excusing others, thankfulness and his own sake, and that he came to complete the noblest qualities of devoutness and humility in his food, garments, drink and dwelling, his eagerness for his family to have faith, and his undertaking the burdens of his Message in helping the religion of Allāh and raising its word, and the injury he met from his people and others which he endured in his homeland and outside of it, some of these qualities are found in the Book of Allāh and books describing him.**

Those who rebelled, who denied, who disbelieved, who rejected, who were hypocrites, were all given respite. They were not destroyed and punishments were not hastened upon them. In fact in one verse, Allāh 🌺 said:

"And Allāh was not to send scourge upon them while you (O Prophet), were in their midst, nor would Allāh send scourge upon them while they are seeking forgiveness."[1]

The verse indicates that while they have two things, they would not be punished. They are:

    i. For as long as the Messenger of Allāh 🌸 is there, Allāh's 🌺 punishment will not descend upon them.

    ii. For as long as they are actively seeking forgiveness, Allāh 🌺 will give them respite and will not punish them. Even the likes of the polytheists of Makkah who would say foul things about Islam were forgiven because they would say, "O Allāh 🌺 forgives us!" as they used to circle around the Kaʿbah.

Looking at the state of the world before his 🌸 arrival, one would say that the world was very close to destruction. If the Messenger of Allāh 🌸 had not come, the world would have descended into chaos and ultimately been destroyed. He was a saviour for the world and a mercy for the entire universe; the humans, the *jinns*, the animals, the birds, the creatures of the sea and even the angels. He once asked Jibrīl 🌸, "How did you benefit from me?" Jibrīl 🌸 replied, "Before you came, I used to fear for my ending. However, when Allāh revealed the Qurʾān to you and praised me, I now have great hope for a good ending."

Shaykh ʿIzz ad-Dīn 🌺 mentions a list of some of his noble qualities and we need to study them so that we too are able to acknowledge what a unique person he was, who was specially chosen by Allāh 🌺.

The statement **"his eagerness for his family to have faith"** can be broadened as he was not just eager for his family to have faith but he was eager for the whole world to believe! He wanted everybody to believe in him and he would spend his nights in prayer, crying to Allāh 🌺. Allāh 🌺 would console him and say:

---

[1] Al-Qurʾān 8:33

"(O Prophet,) perhaps you are going to let yourself collapse in grief because they do not believe."[1]

The Messenger of Allāh's ﷺ Genteleness

31. His gentleness is found in His words, exalted is He, *"It is a mercy from Allāh that you were gentle with them."* (3:159)

This verse is in Sūrah Āle ʿImrān and in reference to the battle of Uḥud where fifty Companions ‎ descended down the hill on which they were positioned. As a result, the enemies attacked the Muslims from behind and they were crushed between the two units of the disbelieving army. After the battle finished, seventy Companions ‎ had been martyred and the Messenger of Allāh ﷺ himself was injured. He was displeased with those who disobeyed his command but was incredibly soft in his discourse with them. Thus, Allāh ‎ revealed the verse:

"So, (O Prophet) it is through mercy from Allāh that you are gentle to them. Had you been rough and hard-hearted, they would have dispersed from around you. So, pardon them, and seek Forgiveness for them. Consult them in the matter and, once you have taken a decision, place your trust in Allāh. Surely, Allāh loves those who place their trust in Him."

After this, the Noble Prophet ﷺ would consult the Companions ‎ who made the mistake whenever they would come to him.

The Messenger of Allāh's ﷺ Mercifulness and Enthusiasm Regarding the Believers

32. His resoluteness against the unbelievers and mercy to the believers is found in His words, exalted is He, *"Muḥammad is the Messenger of Allāh and those who are with him are firm to the unbelievers, merciful to one another."* (48:29)

33. His eagerness for his community to believe, and his compassion for believers and compassion for everyone is found in His words, exalted is He, *"A Messenger has come*

[1] Sūrah Ash Shu'arā 26:3

***to you from among yourselves. Your suffering is distressing to him; he is deeply concerned for you; he is caring and merciful to the believers."* (9:128)**

This shows the eagerness of the Messenger of Allāh ﷺ and his kindness! Allāh is great! Allāh ﷻ called him, "*caring and merciful.*" These are qualities that Allāh ﷻ attributed to Himself but He gave these titles to the Messenger of Allāh ﷺ too.

The Messenger of Allāh's ﷺ Dedication in Conveying the Message

34. His faithfulness in conveying this Message is found in His words, exalted is He, *"Turn away from them, for you are not to blame."* (51:54). If he had fallen short, blame would have been directed at him.

The Messenger of Allāh ﷺ delivered the Message of Allāh ﷻ fully and did not withhold anything. Hence, Allāh ﷻ said, "*Turn away from them, for you are not to blame.*"

ʿĀ'ishah ﷺ once said that if the Noble Prophet ﷺ would have concealed any verse from the Qur'ān, then it would have been the one wherein Allāh ﷻ had said:

> *(Remember) when you (O Prophet,) were saying to the one who was favoured by Allāh and favoured by you, "Keep your wife to yourself, and fear Allāh." And you were concealing in your heart what Allāh was going to reveal, and you were fearing people, while Allāh is more entitled to be feared by you. So, when Zaid finished his desire for her, We gave her into your marriage, so that there may not be a problem for the believers in marrying wives of their adopted sons, when they finish their desire for them; and Allāh's decree had to be enforced."*[1]

There is a story behind this verse; once the Messenger of Allāh ﷺ had instructed Zainab bint Jaḥsh ﷺ to marry Zaid ibn Ḥārithah ﷺ. They married but did not get on well. Zaid ﷺ was very close to the Messenger of Allāh ﷺ and he ﷺ liked him immensely. Zaid ﷺ would regularly come to the Noble Prophet's ﷺ residence and would often complain about Zainab's ﷺ behaviour towards him. The reason for this was because Zaid was a freed slave whereas Zainab ﷺ was a noble woman from the Quraish. They were not compatible because they were from different walks of life. The Messenger of Allāh ﷺ advised him to have patience but then Allāh ﷻ revealed to the

---

[1] Al-Qur'ān 33:37

Noble Prophet ﷺ that Zaid ؓ will soon divorce Zainab ؓ and that she will marry the Messenger of Allāh ﷺ. He was bewildered by this information as Zaid ibn Ḥārithah ؓ was considered his adopted son, a fact that the entire community was aware of. He was even called Zaid ibn Muḥammad ﷺ for a short period of time until Allāh ﷻ forbade this.

During those times, an adopted son was taken as a real son and the people of Ignorance would think it prohibited to marry the wife of their adopted son. The Messenger of Allāh ﷺ was extremely worried about what people may think of him became really afraid as to what people may say. However, in spite of this revelation, the Noble Prophet ﷺ would advise Zaid ؓ "Keep your wife with you! Keep your wife with you!" However, the marriage ended and it was then that Allāh ﷻ commanded the Messenger of Allāh ﷺ to marry Zainab bint Jaḥsh ؓ which he subsequently did.

Thus, this is why ʿĀ'ishah ؓ once said that if the Noble Prophet ﷺ would have concealed any verse from the Qur'ān, then it would have been the one mentioned above. However, he was completely committed to the conveying the Message which is why Shaykh ʿIzz ad-Dīn ؒ said, "**His faithfulness in conveying this Message is found in His words, exalted is He, *"Turn away from them, for you are not to blame."* (51:54). If he had fallen short, blame would have been directed at him."**

The Messenger of Allāh's ﷺ Ummah Will Be Witnesses

35. Another favour is that Allāh, exalted is He, gave his community the ranks of just witnesses with respect to judges. Allāh, exalted is He, gave his community the ranks of just witnesses with respect to judges, for when Allāh, exalted is He, judges between His slaves and the nations deny that the Message was conveyed, the community of Muḥammad ﷺ will be summoned and will testify against people that their messengers conveyed the Message. This quality is not established about any of the prophets.

The *Ummah* will be called as witnesses on Day of Rising. A lengthy ḥadīth is narrated wherein it is mentioned that Nūḥ ؑ will be questioned, "Did you deliver the message?" He will reply affirmatively but his community will belie him and say, "No, he did not!" Allāh ﷻ will say, "Who is your witness O Nūḥ?!" and he will say, "The *Ummah* of Muḥammad ﷺ!"

The *Ummah* will be called and they will say, "We are his witness!" The community of Nūḥ ؑ will ask, "How do you know of this?" and the *Ummah* will reply, "We know through the Qur'ān that was revealed to us by Allāh ﷻ and passed onto us by the Messenger of Allāh ﷺ. Allāh ﷻ speaks the only the truth and He has said that Nūḥ ؑ had delivered the message in Sūrah Nūḥ." Thereafter, the judgement will be made in favour of Nūḥ ؑ.

The Ummah Will Not Unite Upon Misguidance

36. A similar favour is that his community is protected from agreeing on misguidance in either a subsidiary or a central matter.

The Messenger of Allāh ﷺ said, "Allāh would not gather my *Ummah* on error and misguidance."[1] Even if they make a mistake, there will be some amongst them who will guide them. When other nations were led astray, the whole nation went deviated. However, with regards to this nation, Allāh ﷻ has ensured that the *Ummah* will not gather upon deviance.

In another narration it states that Allāh's ﷻ help is with the Congregation [of believers]. This proves that the Companions ؓ are on the right path. Once the Prophet ﷺ said, "Banū Isrā'īl were divided into seventy two sects and my *Ummah* will be divided into seventy three sects all of whom will go into the Fire apart from one." He was asked, "Who are they?" He said, "Those who are upon the path which I and my Companions are upon."

If you look throughout history, different groups and sects have appeared but by the grace of Allāh ﷻ, the majority of the *Ummah* is one. Its example is like that of the ocean, whenever the oil tries to mix with it, it is kept on top and thrown out.

This is why the scholars of Islamic principles have mentioned that the consensus of the *Ummah* is a source of evidence for Sharia rulings. If the Companions ؓ had a consensus, it would have to be used as a source in proving Sharia rulings.

Once al-Imām ash-Shāfiʿī ؒ was asked, "What is the proof that the consensus of the *Ummah* is an evidence? I want the answer from the Qur'ān." Al-Imām ash-Shāfiʿī ؒ began to read the Qur'ān and he read through it in its entirety three times. He kept

[1] Sunan at-Tirmidhī

pondering over its verses and on the third time he came to the verse which proves that the consensus of the *Ummah* is an evidence. He recited the verse:

> *"Whoever breaks away with the Messenger after the right path has become clear to him,* ***and follows what is not the way of the believers,*** *We shall let him have what he chose, and We shall admit him to Jahannam, which is an evil place to return."*[1]

Even today, if the scholars gather upon one ruling then the people will have to follow it as **his community is protected from agreeing on misguidance in either a subsidiary or a central matter.**

The Qur'ān is Protected

37. **Another similar favour is the preservation of His Book. If the first and the last peoples were to agree to add a single word to it or to remove one from it they would be powerless to do that, while the alteration in the Torah and the Gospel is obvious.**

Allāh ﷻ said, "We, Ourselves, have sent down the *Dhikr* (the Qur'ān), and We are there to protect it."[2] Allāh ﷻ has used the 'majestic plural'[3] due to respect. It was the custom of the Arabs that people of high posts would address themselves with the majestic plural and sometimes with the personal pronoun.

With regards to other scriptures, the Messenger of Allāh ﷺ has said that the community it was given too were given the duty of protecting their book. It is for this reason why their books changed when rogue individuals emerged. The pious were unable to repel them and the books were distorted leading to mass interpolation.

On the contrary, the Qur'ān has been protected by Allāh ﷻ through the hearts and minds of numerous individuals. Even today, among the billions of Muslims, you will find millions of those who have memorised the Qur'ān. On the other hand, you will not be able find a single individual who has memorised the previous scriptures. There

---

[1] Al-Qur'ān 4:115

[2] Al-Qur'ān 15:9

[3] The majestic plural; also known as the 'Royal We' or the 'Victorian We' is the use of a plural pronoun to refer to an individual (singular person) who holds a high position.

is not a single person who has memorised the entire Torah, you won't find one! This is why a poet has said:

مسلمانوں نہ گبراہوں خدا کی شان باقی ہے

ابھی اسلام زندہ ہے ابھی قرآن باقی ہے

"O Muslims! Do not be afraid, the majestic nature of Allāh is everlasting,
At present Islam is still alive, at present the Qur'ān still remains."

Another poet said:

نہ ہو ممتاز کیوں اسلام دنیا بھر کے دینوں میں

وہاں مذہب کتابوں میں یہاں قرآن سینوں میں

"Why should Islam not be a distinguished religion from all other religions in the world?
There, their religion is [present] in the books and over here the Qur'ān is [present] in the
hearts and minds."

In Sūrah al-Kahf, wherein the story of Mūsā 🌸 is related, he went to seek knowledge from Khaḍir 🌸 and three incidents occurred. One was that they were travelling on a ship which Khaḍir 🌸 then broke, the second was that he killed a small child and the third was that they came to a city and asked for food but the people were miserly and refused; as they were coming out they saw a wall about to fall but Khaḍir 🌸 solidifed it. Mūsā 🌸 questioned as to why he did this and Khaḍir 🌸 parted ways. In that story, Allāh 🌸 said:

"Then, they moved ahead until they came to the people of a town; they asked its people for food, and they refused to host them."[1]

The exegetes of the Qur'ān highlight that people came to 'Umar 🌸 from the city of Intāqiya, the people of the town mentioned in the verse, and said, "With regards to

---

[1] Al-Qur'ān 18:77

the mention of our town in the Qur'ān where it is stated, '*they refused to host them* أَن يُضَيِّفُوهُمَا. Can you change the dot below the '*bā*' and add two dots above it to make a '*tā*' so it reads فَأَتَوْا أن يُضَيِّفُوهُمَا - *they came forth and served them*."

All they had to do was change the dots and would receive praise for the city. ʿUmar ﷺ was ʿUmar ﷺ and so he showed his fury and said, "Get out of here! I cannot change the Qur'ān!" It is impossible for the Qur'ān to be changed. It has been preserved within the breasts and hearts of the believers and it cannot be changed.

Allāh ﷻ Concealed The Ummah's Rejected Deeds

38. Another is that Allāh concealed those of his community whose actions are not accepted, while when earlier nations offered sacrifices, fire would consume those which were accepted and leave behind what was not accepted so that the person was disgraced.

Allāh says for that reason: *"We have only sent you as a mercy to all the worlds."*(21:107) and the Prophet ﷺ said, "I am a guiding mercy" and, "I am the Prophet of mercy."

If a person of a previous nation committed fornication or theft, it would be written on their home the following morning. Allāh ﷻ has concealed the faults of this *Ummah* and gave us respite so that we can seek forgiveness from Allāh ﷻ from Him.

The Messenger of Allāh ﷺ Was Gifted With Great Oration

39. Another is that he was sent with concise but comprehensive words, and speech was made very succinct for him, and he excelled the Arabs in his eloquence and expressiveness.

For example, the Messenger of Allāh ﷺ said, "Actions are but by intentions"[1] and "A complete believer is he from whose hands and tongue others feel safe."[2]

The Messenger of Virtue ﷺ

40. As Allāh favoured him over His human prophets and messengers, He similarly

---

[1] Ṣaḥīḥ al-Bukḥārī

[2] Ibid

favoured him over those He chose from His messengers among the heavenly beings and His angels, although the highest ranking humans are better than the angels according to His words, exalted is He, *"Those who believe and do right actions: they are the best of creatures."* (98:7) Angels are counted among 'creatures (bariyyah)' because 'bariyyah' is derived from, "Allāh created (bara'a) the creation," i.e., originated and brought into existence. Angels are not included in His words, exalted is He, *"Those who believe and do right actions"* although they believe and do right actions, because this expression is normally used for those of mankind who believe as if evidenced by the fact that it is what usually comes to mind first. It is said that bariyyah is derived from al-bara, which is earth and the human being is created from earth so it is as if he said, "Those who believe and do right actions, those are the best of human beings."

Shaykh ʿIzz ad-Dīn is talking about the verse of Sūrah Bayyinah where Allāh said: *"Those who believe and work righteous deeds, they are the best among the creation."*[1]

Shaykh ʿIzz ad-Dīn is indicating that those who believe and work righteous deeds are the best among creation which include angels and mankind. Thus, the leader of mankind is the Messenger of Allāh and so he will be the best among the creation whether it is mankind or the angels.

Now, the book is going into the literal meaning of the word 'bariyyah' and where it originates. This does not concern us so we will leave these few paragraphs. Here, Shaykh ʿIzz ad-Dīn is only giving an answer to objections made by other people.

These are indications and glimpses whose like are sufficient for the person of intellect. Rather even some of them are sufficient.

We ask Allāh, exalted is He, by His favour and generosity to grant us success in following His Messenger in His *sunnah* and path and all his character, both outward and inward, and to place us among his party and helpers. He has power over all things and is worthy of the answer. There is no power or strength except by Allāh, the High, the Immense.

---

[1] Al-Qurʾān 98:7

May Allāh bless our master Muḥammad and his family and Companions and g
them abundant peace constantly and always.

This is the end of the '*Bidāyah As-Sūl Fī Tafḍīl Ar-Rasūl*', and praise belongs to Allāh alone.

Arabic text of Bidāyah As-Sūl Fī Tafḍīl Ar-Rasūl

بسم الله الرحمن الرحيم

رَبِّ يَسِّرْ وأعِنْ يا كَرِيْم

قال الشيخ الإمام ، العالم العلامة عز الدين أبو محمد عبد العزيز بن عبد السلام بن أبي القاسم السلمي الشافعي ، رحمه الله تعالى وغفر له :

الحمد لله الذي خلق الإنسان ، وفضّله بالأصغرينِ القلبِ واللسان ، وأحمدُهُ على ما علّم من البيان ، وأشكره على ما أَوْلى من الإحسان .

وأشهد أن لا إله الا الله وحدَهُ لا شريك له ، شهادةً أرجو بها الفوزَ والإيمان وأشهد أنَّ محمّداً عبدهُ ورسولُهُ المصطفى من بني عدنان ، المؤيَّد بالمعجزات الظاهرات والقرآن ، و الأنوار الباهرات و البرهان ، المفضَّلُ على سائر المخلوقات : من الملائكة والإنس و الجان ، صلى الله عليهِ وعلى آله ما ائتلفَ الشَّكلانِ ، واختلف الضّدّانِ .

و بعد :

فإنّي التمستُ من والدي – أعزّه اللهُ بالإسلام أن يُمليَ عليَّ شيئاً في تفضيل النّبيِ – صلى الله عليه وسلَّم – على جميع الأنام ، فأجابني من غير توقُّفٍ ولا إحجام .

فقال : قال الله تعالى لنبيّنا صلواتُ الله عليه وسلامه مُتمنّناً عليه ، مُعرِّفاً لقَدْره لديه : ﴿ وَأَنزَلَ اللَّهُ

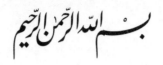

عَلَيْكَ الْكِتَابَ وَالْحِكْمَةَ وَعَلَّمَكَ مَا لَمْ تَكُن تَعْلَمُ ۚ وَكَانَ فَضْلُ اللَّهِ عَلَيْكَ عَظِيمًا ﴾

وقد فضَّل اللهُ بعضَ الرُّسول على بعضٍ : ﴿ مِّنْهُم مَّن كَلَّمَ اللَّهُ ۖ وَرَفَعَ بَعْضَهُمْ دَرَجَاتٍ ۚ ﴾ ؛ التفضيلُ الأولُ : صريحٌ في أصلِ المفاضلة ، والثاني : في تضعيفِ المفاضلة بدرجاتٍ ، ونكَّرها تنكيرَ التعظيمِ بمعنى درجاتٍ أيِّ درجاتٍ ؟!

و قد فضَّل اللهُ سبحانَهُ وتعالى نبيَّنا محمداً صلَّى الله عليه و سلَّم من وجوهٍ :

١ - اولها : انه ساد الكل قال صلى الله عليه و سلّم : ((انا سيّد ولد آدم يوم القيامة و لا فخر)) والسيّدُ مَن اتصف بالصفات العليّة ، والأخلاق السنيّة . وهذا مشعرٌ بأنه أفضلُ منهم فى الدارين ، أمّا في الدنيا فلما اتصَفَ به من الأخلاق العظيمة . وأمّا في الآخرةِ فلأن الجزاءَ مرتّبٌ على الأخلاق والأوصاف ، فإذا فَضَلَهم في الدنيا في المناقب والصفات ، فَضَلَهم في الآخرة في المراتب والدرجات . وإنما قال صلى الله عليه وسلّم :((أنا سيد ولد آدم ولا فخر)) لتعرف أمتُه منزلته من ربه عزّ وجل ، ولمّا كان ذكر مناقب النفس إنما تذكر افتخاراً في الغالب ، أراد صلى الله عليه وسلّم أن يقطع وَهمَ من توهم من الجهلة أن يذكر ذلك افتخاراً فقال : ((و لا فخر)) .

٢ - ومنها قوله صلى الله عليه وسلّم : ((وبيدي لواء الحمد يوم القيامة ولا فخر)) .

٣ - و منها قوله صلى الله عليه وسلّم : ((آدم فمن دونه تحت لوائي يوم القيامة ولا فخر)) .

و هذه الخصائص تدل على علو مرتبته إذ لا معنى للتفضيل الا التخصيص بالمناقب و المراتب .

٤ - ومنها أن الله تعالى أخبره بأنه غفر له ما تقدم من ذنبه وما تأخر ، ولم ينقل أنه أخبر أحداً من الأنبياء بمثل ذلك ، بل الظاهر أنه لم يخبرهم ، لأن كل واحد منهم إذا طُلبَتْ منهم الشفاعة في الموقف ذكر خطيئته التي أصابها وقال : ((نفسي نفسي)) ولو علم كل واحد منهم بغفران خطيئته لم يُوْجَل منها في ذلك المقام ، وإذا استشفعت الخلائق بالنبي صلى الله عليه وسلّم في ذلك المقام قال: ((أنا لها)) .

٥ – ومنها أنه صلى الله عليه وسلّم اوّل شافع و اوّل مشفّع و هذا يدل على تخصيصه و تفضيله .

٦- ومنها إيثاره صلى الله عليه وسلّم على نفسه ، إذ جعل لكل نبي دعوة مستجابة ، فكل منهم تعجل دعوته في الدنيا ، واختبأ هو صلى الله عليه وسلّم دعوته شفاعةً لأمَّتِهِ .

٧ - ومنها أن الله تعالى أقسم بحياته صلى الله عليه وسلّم فقال ﴿ لَعَمْرُكَ إِنَّهُمْ لَفِي سَكْرَتِهِمْ يَعْمَهُونَ ﴾ والإقسام بحياةِ المُقْسَم بحياته يدل على شرق بحياته وعِزَّتها عند المُقْسِم بها وأن حياته صلى الله عليه وسلّم لجديرة أن يقسم بها لما فيها من البركة العامة والخاصة ، ولم يثبت هذا لغيره صلى الله عليه وسلّم.

٨ – ومنها أن الله تعالى وقَّره في ندائه ، فناداهُ بأحبِّ أسمائه وأسني أوصافه فقال: ﴿ يَا أَيُّهَا النَّبِيُّ ﴾ ، و﴿ يَا أَيُّهَا الرَّسُوْلُ ﴾ وهذه الخصيصة لم تثبت لغيره ، بل ثبت أنَّ كلاً منهم نودي باسمه ، فقال تعالي: ﴿ يَا آدَمُ اسْكُنْ ﴾ ، ﴿ يَا عِيسَى ابْنَ مَرْيَمَ اذْكُرْ نِعْمَتِي عَلَيْكَ ﴾ ، ﴿ يَٰمُوسَىٰٓ إِنِّىٓ أَنَا ٱللَّهُ ﴾ ، ﴿ يَا نُوحُ اهْبِطْ بِسَلَامٍ مِّنَّا ﴾ ، ﴿ يَا دَاوُودُ إِنَّا جَعَلْنَاكَ خَلِيفَةً فِي الْأَرْضِ ﴾ ، ﴿ يَا إِبْرَاهِيمُ قَدْ صَدَّقْتَ الرُّؤْيَا ﴾ ، ﴿ يَٰلُوطُ إِنَّا رُسُلُ رَبِّكَ ﴾ ، ﴿ يَا زَكَرِيَّا إِنَّا نُبَشِّرُكَ ﴾ ، ﴿ يَا يَحْيَىٰ خُذِ الْكِتَابَ بِقُوَّةٍ ﴾

ولا يخفى على أحد أن السيد إذا دَعى أحدَ عبيده بأفضل ما وجد فيهم من الأوصاف العليَّة والأخلاق السنيَّة ، ودعا الآخرين بأسمائهم الأعلام لا يُشعر بوصف من الأوصاف ، ولا بخُلُق من الأخلاق ، أنَّ منزلة من دعاه بأفضل الأسماء والأوصاف أعزّ عليه وأقرب إليه ممن دعاه باسمه العلم . وهذا معلومٌ بالعرف أن من دُعي بأفضل أوصافه وأخلاقه كل ذلك مبالغة في تعظيمه واحترامه ، حتى قال قائل :

لا تدعنى إلا بيا عبدَها   فإنه افضل أسمائي .

٩ – ومنها أن معجزة كل نبي تصرَّمت وانقرضت ، ومعجزة سيد الأولين والآخرين وهي القرآن العظيم باقيةً إلى يوم الدين .

١٠ – ومنها تسليم الحجر عليه ، وحنين الجذع إليه ولم يثبت لواحد من الأنبياء مثل ذلك . خذ ما تراه ودع شيئاً سمعت به .

١١ - ومنها أنه وجد في معجزاته ما هو أظهر في الإعجاز من معجزات غيره ، كتفجير الماء من بين أصابعه . فإنه أبلغ في خرق العادة من تفجيره من الحَجر ، لأن جنس الأحجار مما يتفجر منه الماء ، وكانت معجزته بانفجار الماء من بين أصابعه أبلغ من انفجار الحجر لموسى عليه السلام .

١٢ – و منها أن عيسى عليه السلام أبرأ الأكمَه مع بقاء عينه في مقّرها ، و رسول الله صلى الله عليه و سلّم ردَّ العين بعد أن سالت على الخَدّ . ففيه معجزة من وجهين :

احدهما : التئآمها بعد سيلانها ،

و الأخرى : رد البصر إليها بعد فقده منها .

١٣ - و منها أن الأموات الذين أحياهم من الكفر بالإيمان أكثر عدداً ممن أحياهم عيسى حياة الأبدان . و سيأتي بيان حياة الإيمان و حياة الأبدان .

١٤ - ومنها أن الله تعالى يكتب لكل نبي من الأنبيآء من الأجر بقدر أعْمال أمته وأحوالها وأقوالها ؛ وأمَّتُهُ شطر أهل الجنة ، وقد أخبر الله تعالى أن أمَّته خير أمةٍ أخرجت للناس ، وإنما كانوا خير الأمم لما اتصفوا به من المعارف والأحوال والأقوال و الأعمال ، فما من معرفة ولا حالة ولا عبادة ولا مقالة ولا شيء مما يتقرب به إلى الله عزَّ و جل مّما دل عليه رسول الله صلى الله عليه و سلّم و دعى إليه إلاّ و له أجر من عمل به إلى يوم القيامة ، ولا يَبْلُغ احدٌ من الأبياء إلى هذه المرتبة . و قد جاء في الحديث : ((الخلق عيال الله ، و أحبهم إليه أنفعهم لعياله)) . فإذا كان صلى الله عليه و سلّم قد نفع شطر أهل الجنة ، و غيره من الأنبيآء إنما نفع جزءاً من أجزاء الشطر ، كانت منزلته صلى الله عليه و سلّم ، في القرب على قدر منزلة في النفع ، فما من عارف من أمته إلا وله مثل اجر معرفته مضافاً إلى معارفه صلى الله عليه و سلّم ، و ما من ذي حال من أمته إلا وله صلى الله عليه و سلّم مثل اجره على حاله مضموماً إلى أحواله صلى الله عليه و سلّم ، و ما من ذي مقال يُتَقَرَّبُ به إلى الله عزَّ و جل إلا وله صلى الله عليه و سلّم مثل اجر ذلك

القول مضموماً إلى مقالته و تبليغ رسالته ، وما من عمل من الأعمال المقربة إلى الله عزَّ وجل من صلوةٍ وزكاةٍ وعتقٍ وجهادٍ وبرٍ ومعروفٍ وذكرٍ وصبرٍ وعفوٍ وصفحٍ إلا وله صلى الله عليه و سلّم مثل اجر عامله مضموماً إلى اجره على أعماله ، وما من درجةٍ عَلِيَّةٍ ، ومرتبةٍ سنيَّةٍ ، نالها احد امَّتِهِ بإرشاده و دلالته إلا وله مثل اجرها مضموماً إلى درجته صلى الله عليه و سلّم ومرتبته ، ويتضاعف ذلك بأن من دعى من امَّتِهِ إلى هدىً أو سنَّ سنة حسنة كان له اجر من عمل بالك على عدد العاملين ، ثم يكون هذا المضاعف لنبيّنا صلى الله عليه وسلّم ، لانه دل عليه ، وأرشد عليه ، ولأجل هذا بكى موسى عليه السلام ليلة الإسراء بكاء غِبطةٍ غَبَطَ بها النبي صلى الله عليه و سلّم ، اذ يدخل من أمته الجنّة أكثر مما يدخل من أمة موسى عليه السلام و لم يبك حسداً كما يتوهمه بعض الجهال ، و إنما بكا أسفاً على ما فاته من مثل مرتبته.

١٥ – ومنها أن الله أرسل كل نبي إلى قومه خاصة ، وأرسل نبينا محمداً صلى الله عليه وسلّم إلى الجن والإنس ، ولكل نبي من الأنبياء ثواب تبليغه إلى أمته ، ولنبينا صلى الله عليه وسلّم ثواب التبليغ إلى كل من أرسل إليه ، تارة لمباشرة الإبلاغ ، وتارة بالنسبة إليه ولذلك تمنّن عليه بقوله تعالى: ﴿ وَلَوْ شِئْنَا لَبَعَثْنَا فِي كُلِّ قَرْيَةٍ نَّذِيرًا ﴾ ، ووجه التمنّن : أنه لو بعث في كل قريةٍ نذيراً لما حصل لرسول الله صلى الله عليه وسلّم إلاّ أجر إنذاره لأهل قريته .

١٦ – ومنها أن الله تعالى كلَّم موسى عليه السلام بالطور، وبالوادي المقدَّس ، وكلّم نبيّنا صلى الله عليه وسلّم عند سدرة المنتهى .

١٧ – ومنها أنه قال : ((نحن الآخرون من أهل الدنيا والأولون يوم القيامة ، المقضي لهم قبل الخلائق ، ونحن أول من يدخل الجنة)) .

١٨ – ومنها أنه لما ذكر السؤدد مطلقا فقد قيَّده بـ ((يوم القيامة وأوّل من ينشق عنه القبر ، وأوّل شافع و انا اوّل مشفّع)) .

١٩ – ومنها أنه صلى الله عليه وسلّم أخبر أنه يرغب إليه الخلق كلهم يوم القيامة ، حتى إبراهيم .

٢٠ – ومنها أنه يدخل من أمَّتِهِ إلى الجنّةِ سبعون ألفاً بغير حساب ولم يثبت ذلك لغيره صلى الله عليه وسلّم .

٢١ – ومنها أنه قال : ((الوسيلة منزلة في الجنة لا ينبغي أن تكون إلا لعبد من عباد الله تعالى ، وارجوا أن أكون أنا هو ، فمن سأل لي الوسيلة حلّت عليه الشفاعة)) .

٢٢ – ومنها : الكوثر الذي أعطيه ففي الجنة ، والحوض الذي أعطيه في الموقف .

٢٣ – ومنها قوله صلى الله عليه وسلم : ((نحن الآخرون السابقون)) الآخرون زماناً ، السابقون بالمناقب والفضائل.

٢٤ – ومنها أنه أُحلّت له الغنائم ولم تحل لأحدٍ قبله ، وجعلت صفوف أمَّتِهِ كصفوف الملائكة ، وجعلت له الأرض مسجداً ، وترابها طهوراً . وهذه الخصائص تدل على علوّ مرتبته ، والرفق بأمَّتِهِ .

٢٥ – ومنها أن الله تعالى أثنى على خُلُقه فقال : ﴿ وَإِنَّكَ لَعَلَىٰ خُلُقٍ عَظِيمٍ ﴾ ، واستعظام العظماء للشيء يدل على إيغاله في العَظَمة ، فما الظن باستعظام أعظم العظماء ؟

٢٦ – ومنها أن الله تعالى كَلَّمَهُ بأنواع الوحي وهي ثلاثة :

أحدها : الرؤيا الصادقة .

والثاني : الكلام من غير واسطة .

والثالث : مع جبريل صلى الله عليه وسلّم .

٢٧ – ومنها أن كتابة صلى الله عليه وسلّم مشتمل على ما اشتملت عليه التوراة والإنجيل والزبور ، وفُضِّل بالمفصّل .

٢٨ – ومنها أن أمَّتَهُ أقل عملاً ممن قبلهم ، وأكثر أجراً كما جاء في الحديث الصحيح .

٢٩ – ومنها أن الله عزّ وجلّ عرض عليه مفاتيح كنوز الأرض وخيَّرهُ أن يكون ملكاً أو نبيّاً عبداً ، فاستشار جبريل عليه السلام . فأشار إليه أن تواضعْ . فقال له : ((نبيّاً عبداً ، أجوع يوماً ، و أشبع يوماً ، فإذا جعتُ دعوت الله ، و إذا شبعتُ شكرت الله)) ؛ قصد صلى الله عليه وسلّم ان يكون مشغولاً بالله في طورَي الشدة و الرخاء ، و النعمة و البلاء .

٣٠ – ومنها أن الله تعالى أرسله (رحمةً للعالمين) ، فأمهل عصاة أمته ولم يعاجلهم إبقاء عليهم ، بخلاف من تقدمه من الأنبياء فإنهم لما كُذِّبوا عوجل مكذبهم . وأمَّا أخْلاقُهُ صلى الله عليه وسلّم في حلمه وعفوه وصفحه وصبره وشكره ولينه في الله ، وانه لم يغضب لنفسه ، وأنه جاء بإتمام مكارم الأخلاق ، وما نقل من خشوعه وخضوعه وتَبُّتله وتواضعه في مأكله ، وملبسة ، ومشربه ، ومسكنه ، وجميل عشرته ، وكريم خليقَته ، وحسن سجيَّته ، ونصحه لأمتِهِ ، وحرصه على إيمان عشيرته ، وقيامه بأعباء رسالته في نصرة دين الله ، وإعلاء كلمته ، وما لقيه من أذى قومه وغيرهم في وطنه وغربته ، فبعض هذه المناقب موجودة في كتاب الله وكتب شمائله .

٣١ – أمَّا لينُه ففي قوله تعالى : ﴿ فَبِمَا رَحْمَةٍ مِّنَ اللَّهِ لِنتَ لَهُمْ ﴾

٣٢ – وأمَّا شدَّته على الكافرين ، ورحمته على المؤمنين ففي قوله تعالى : ﴿ مُّحَمَّدٌ رَّسُولُ اللَّهِ ۚ وَالَّذِينَ مَعَهُ أَشِدَّاءُ عَلَى الْكُفَّارِ رُحَمَاءُ بَيْنَهُمْ ﴾

٣٣ – وأمَّا حرصه على إيمان أمَّتِهِ ، ورأفته بالمؤمنين ، وشفقته على الكافة ففي قوله تعالى : ﴿لَقَدْ جَاءَكُمْ رَسُولٌ مِّنْ أَنفُسِكُمْ عَزِيزٌ عَلَيْهِ مَا عَنِتُّمْ أي يُشق عليه ما يشق عليكم ، ۞ حَرِيصٌ عَلَيْكُم أي إيمانكم ۞ بِالْمُؤْمِنِينَ رَءُوفٌ رَّحِيمٌ ﴾

٣٤ – وأمَّا نصحه في أداء رسالته ففي قوله تعالى : ﴿ فَتَوَلَّ عَنْهُمْ فَمَا أَنتَ بِمَلُومٍ ﴾ و لو اقتصر لتوجه عليه اللوم .

٣٥ – ومنها أن الله تعالى نزَّل أمَّته منزل العدول من الحكام ، فإن الله تعالى إذا حكم بين العباد فجحدت الأمم بتبليغ الرسالة أحضر أمَّةَ محمد صلى الله عليه وسلّم فيشهدون على الناس بأن رسلهم أبلغتهم ، وهذه الخصيصة لم تثبت لأحد من الأنبياء .

٣٦ – ومثلها عصمة أمَّتِهِ بأنها لا تجتمع على ضلالةٍ ، في فرعٍ ولا في أصل.

٣٧ – ومثلها حفظ كتابه ، فَلَوْ اجتمع الأولون و الآخرون على أن يزيدوا فيه كلمة ، أو ينقصوا منه لعجزوا عن ذلك ، ولا يخفى ما وقع من التبديل في التوراة والإنجيل.

٣٨ – ومنها أن الله ستر على من لم يتقبل عمله من أمَّتِهِ ، و كان من قبلهم يقرِّبون القرابين ، فتأكل النار ما تقبل منها ، و تدع ما لم يتقبَّل ، فيصبح مفتضحاً و لمثل ذلك قال الله : ﴿ وَمَا أَرْسَلْنَاكَ إِلَّا رَحْمَةً لِّلْعَالَمِينَ ﴾ و قال صلى الله عليه و سلّم : ((انّما انا رحمة مهداةٌ)) ((أنا نبي الرحمة)) .

٣٩ – ومنها أنه بعث بجوامع الكلم ، واختصر له الحديث اختصاراً ، وفاق العَرَب في فصاحته وبلاغته.

٤٠ – و كما فضّله الله على أنبيائه و رسله من البشر فكذلك فضله على من اصطفاه من رسله من اهل السماء و ملائكته لقوله تعالى : ﴿ إِنَّ الَّذِينَ آمَنُوا وَعَمِلُوا الصَّالِحَاتِ أُولَٰئِكَ هُمْ خَيْرُ الْبَرِيَّةِ ﴾ و الملائكة من جملة البرية ؛ لأن (الْبَرِيَّة) مأخوذة من (برأ الله الخلق) أي اخترعه و أوجده ، و لا تدخل الملائكة في قوله تعالى ﴿ إِنَّ ٱلَّذِينَ ءَامَنُواْ وَعَمِلُواْ ٱلصَّٰلِحَٰتِ ﴾ ، مع أنهم قد آمنوا وعملوا الصالحات ، لأن هذه اللفظة تختص بعرف الإستعمال بمن آمن من البشر ، بدليل أنه المتبادر إلى الأفهام عند الإطلاق ، فإن قيل : البرية مأخوذة من (البرا) و هو التراب ، و البشر مخلوق من التراب لكأنه قال : إنّ الّذين ءامنوا وعملوا الصٰلحٰت أولَئك هم خير البشر . فالجواب من وجهين :

أحدها : أن أئمة اللغة قد عددوا البرية في جملة ما تركت العرب همزهُ .

والوجه ثاني وهو الأظهر : أن نافعاً قرأ بالهمز ، وكلا القراءتين كلام الله ، فإن كانت إحدى القراءتين قد فضّلت الذين آمنوا على سائر البشر . وإذا ثبت أن أفاضل البشر أفضل من الملائكة ، فالانبياء صلوات

الله عليهم أفضل ٱلَّذِينَ ءَامَنُواْ وَعَمِلُواْ ٱلصَّٰلِحَٰتِ بدليل قوله تعالى بعد ذكر جماعة من الأنبياء ﴿ وَكُلًّا فَضَّلْنَا عَلَى الْعَالَمِينَ ﴾ فدلت هذه الآية على أنهم أفضل البشر من الملائة ، لأن الملائكة من (العالَمين) سواء كان مشتقاً من العلم أو من العلامة ، وإذا كانت الأنبياء أفضلَ من الملائكة فرسول الله صلى الله عليه وسلّم أفضلُ الأنبياء ، فقد ساد ساداتِ الملائكة ، فصار أفضل من الملائكة بدرجتين ، و أعلا منهم برتبتين ، لا يعلم قدر تلك الرتبتين وشرف تلك الدرجتين إلاّ من فضّل خاتم النبيين ، وسيّد المرسلين على جميع العالمين . وهذه لمع وإشارات يكتفي العاقل الفطن بمثلها بل ببعضها.

ونحن نسأل الله بمنه وكرمه أن يوفقنا لإتباع رسوله في سننه وطريقته ، وجميع أخلاقه الظاهرة والباطنة ، وأن يجعلنا من أحزابه وأنصاره . إن الله على كل شيء قدير و بالإجابة جدير ، ولا حول ولا قوة إلا بالله العظيم .

وصلى الله على سيّدنا محمد وعلى آله وصحبه وسلم تسليما كثيراً دائماً أبداً.

آخر ((بداية السول في تفضيل الرسول)) والحمد لله وحده .

Notes

Notes

Notes

Notes

Notes